AF553835

Be Unique,
The Flipkart Way

Be Unique, The Flipkart Way

Unravelling Unprecedented Corporate Entrepreneurship

VARADHARAJU JANARDHANAN
and M.H. BALA SUBRAHMANYA

RUPA

Published by
Rupa Publications India Pvt. Ltd 2024
7/16, Ansari Road, Daryaganj
New Delhi 110002

Sales centres:
Bengaluru Chennai Hyderabad
Jaipur Kathmandu Kolkata
Mumbai Prayagraj

Any views or opinions presented in this book are solely those of the authors. Any information, figures or numbers mentioned in the book are sourced by the authors from the public domain and are based on research undertaken by the authors. Flipkart accepts no liability for the contents of this book, or for the consequences of any actions taken on the basis of the information contained therein. This book represents the personal views of the authors and opinions formed based on the research undertaken by the authors and does not necessarily reflect the positions or opinions of Flipkart with whom the authors are affiliated. The content presented herein is based on the authors' analysis, perspectives and interpretation of the subject matter.

The views and opinions expressed in this book are the authors' own and the facts are as reported by them, which have been verified to the extent possible, and the publishers are not in any way liable for the same.

P-ISBN: 978-93-6156-204-4
E-ISBN: 978-93-6156-505-2

First impression 2024

10 9 8 7 6 5 4 3 2 1

Printed in India

CONTENTS

LIST OF TABLES

LIST OF FIGURES

FOREWORD

Most academic research is based on regression-driven correlations, not cause-and-effect correlations. Seldom do we come across research from the data of practitioners that correlates cause and effect.

This research about Flipkart, a jewel of India, is a rare foray into corporate entrepreneurship in emerging economies and the start-up arena. Sustained entrepreneurship in a corporation is caused by executives and managers who believe in it and actively take entrepreneurship initiatives. They regularly create internal teams to carry these out, provide resources, build ecosystems, support ex-employees to build start-ups; and the board monitors them.

The authors have meticulously correlated entrepreneurial initiatives that were shaped, monitored and executed, with the creation of market value. This is what I call practical qualitative research, clearly correlating cause and effect. It demonstrates that the traditional belief of corporate entrepreneurship that a separate venture fund will create is no longer the best option.

I highly recommend this book to students, professors,

researchers, management consultants, incubators and corporate executives and believe that they will find this research highly useful.

Ram Charan

Ram Charan is a world-renowned business consultant, author and speaker who has spent the past 50 years working with many top companies, CEOs, and boards of our time. He is advisor to Flipkart and has advised other CEOs in GE, Dupont, Bank of America, Aditya Birla, and the Adani Group, as well as boards in China, Brazil, and the USA.

Ram Charan has authored more than 36 books, including *The New York Times* bestselling book *Execution*.

PREFACE

Tech start-ups hold significant promise for the future in developed as well as emerging economies. They act as potential sources of innovations, offering solutions to a wide range of human problems. Additionally, they contribute to economic growth by generating employment, income and exports. Accordingly, they increasingly attract attention in terms of public policy support to nurture start-up ecosystems.

However, the high failure rate of start-ups (about 90%) has not subsided, despite a steady increase in policy support extended by governments to start-up creation and their growth across the globe. Given this scenario, it is imperative for new and existing start-ups to derive lessons from the few successful ones, and for governments to fine-tune public policies for start-ups.

In the global economy today, India is considered one of the 'front-line' economies in terms of start-up hubs, number of start-ups and start-up exits. Today, almost every state in India has an exclusive 'start-up policy'. The Government of India has increasingly emphasised promoting start-ups by developing infrastructure and ecosystems that include support systems in terms of Technology Business Incubators (TBIs), mentors, venture capital funds, and facilitating entrepreneurship.

However, the failure rate of start-ups in India is no different from that of the rest of the world. This poses two questions: how can the start-up failure rate be mitigated, and secondly, how can a larger proportion of start-ups be enabled to steadily succeed and grow?

To respond to these challenges, we need to learn lessons from a few successful ones. Bangalore (also known as Bengaluru) in India is an internationally recognized start-up hub and has an ever-evolving start-up ecosystem. It has a significant concentration of emerging and sustaining start-ups, including a few 'scaled-up' ones. Notably, Flipkart stands apart from most other start-ups in India.

Flipkart emerged as a tech start-up in the e-commerce industry in Bangalore in 2007. Back then, both the infrastructure necessary for e-commerce to flourish and consumer familiarity with online shopping were severely lacking. Flipkart was founded by two young IIT Delhi graduates, Binny Bansal and Sachin Bansal, who had little to no prior entrepreneurial experience, neither from their families nor from their professional lives. They had not visited the 'Mecca of Start-ups', Silicon Valley in the USA, or indeed, any other developed start-up ecosystem, to gain exposure to start-ups or the elements of a start-up ecosystem. As such, both were naive entrepreneurs, who were relatively unaware about the enormous challenges in setting up a start-up and operating it for sustenance and growth.

How did the founders navigate challenges in technical and financial aspects, securing funding, marketing strategy, attracting talent, finding mentors, and building a network? How did Flipkart successfully overcome the 'valley of death' in a short span of time to become a unicorn by 2012? How did it achieve stability and steady success, registering unprecedented growth over time since then, to emerge as one of the largest e-commerce companies in India?

We delve into these key questions through in-depth empirical research work spanning nearly 15 years, from 2007-2022. We firmly believe that the exploration of factors that contributed to the "unprecedented growth story of Flipkart" holds key lessons for other tech start-ups and prospective start-up founders in India and beyond. We carried out this research with utmost attention and diligence to help the start-up ecosystem in general, and Indian start-up ecosystem in particular. We fondly hope that our work will add value, influencing both start-up policy as much as start-up practice.

Varadharaju Janardhanan
M.H. Bala Subrahmanya

Bengaluru

1

INTRODUCTION

Backdrop

India occupies a unique position as a potential source of tech entrepreneurship-based start-ups in the global start-up landscape (Gai and Joffe, 2013; Bala Subrahmanya, 2021). India has the third-largest start-up ecosystem in the world today (Startup India, 2022). Justifiably, Europe's biggest start-up and technology conference, Viva Technology Conference, in its sixth edition held during 15–18 June 2022 in Paris, France, identified India as the 'country of the year' in view of its remarkable performance on the global start-up landscape (Davies, 2022). India has at least six start-up hubs which have a global recognition today (Start-up Genome, 2022). Among these, Bangalore stands apart as one of the leading start-up hubs in the global start-up landscape. In addition, Bangalore has obtained multiple global recognitions such as the 'Silicon Valley of India', 'cluster of R&D affiliates', and as an 'innovation cluster' (Bala Subrahmanya, 2020).

All this has been facilitated by a strong and ever-increasing base of science and technology professionals and a favourable policy environment (Bala Subrahmanya, 2021). The policy support extended by the Government of India has played a unique role in promoting start-up ecosystems and tech start-ups in the country. The first-ever policy document that made explicit reference to start-ups and proposed policy support was the recommendations of the Inter-Ministerial Committee for Accelerating Manufacturing in Micro, Small and Medium Enterprises Sector in 2013. The Inter-Ministerial Committee proposed several measures to strengthen financial support for start-ups (Bala Subrahmanya, 2018). Subsequently, the Government of India launched an exclusive Start-up India Action Plan in January 2016 (Department of Industrial Policy and Promotion, 2016). The new start-up policy primarily focussed on regulatory issues, funding support and incentives, the promotion of industry–academia partnerships, and incubation centres. Concurrently, several state governments, including the Government of Karnataka, formulated their own start-up promotion policies at the state level (Bala Subrahmanya, 2018). All this laid a foundation for the emergence and growth of start-up ecosystems and growth of tech start-ups into unicorns, leading to the generation of employment and income in the country.

Both due to a strong and growing S&T workforce base and consistent policy support, Bangalore emerged as the leading tech start-up hub in the country. Named the 'start-up capital of India' from the beginning of 2010s, Bangalore continues to be recognized as such till today.

In terms of unicorns (privately held start-up companies with a valuation of more than $1 billion), as of 2022, India ranks third globally (behind the United States and China), and Bangalore accounts for almost half of India's total, indicating the dominance that Bangalore entrepreneurial ecosystem has in the country's start-up landscape (Davies, 2022; Bala Subrahmanya, 2022). In fact, Bangalore is the centre of India's high-tech industry and is considered India's unicorn capital with the largest number of unicorn headquarters (Invest India, 2022). [A description on the Unicorns in India is presented in Annexure 1.1.]

Among the unicorns, Flipkart is one of the earliest and one of the largest which has been playing an important role in strengthening the start-up ecosystem of India in general, and that of Bangalore, in particular. Perhaps Flipkart was one of the early ones to attain the status of a decacorn in India (a company that has attained a valuation of >$ 10 billion) (Invest India, Crunchbase, 2021). Since its founding in 2007, Flipkart has emerged as one of the largest e-commerce players in India today.

In the process of its growth, it has absorbed many tech start-ups through mergers and acquisitions (M&A) and at the same time, generated several tech start-ups. These have been through ex-Flipsters, as former Flipkart executives are called, some of whom became unicorns as well. Moreover, Flipsters encourage the emergence and growth of multiple start-ups in the Indian start-up ecosystem as investors and mentors, among others. Thus, Flipkart has defined a distinctly unique growth path for future tech start-ups in India over a period of time.

The growth experience of Flipkart is, therefore, unprecedented and unparalleled in India's start-up ecosystem and new technology industry history (Dalal, 2019a). This assumes significance because e-commerce had hardly developed in India when Flipkart emerged in the late 2000s. Even the start-up ecosystem in the country, including Bangalore, was just evolving almost after a decade (Bala Subrahmanya, 2017). The prevalent internet infrastructure then was hardly adequate for the growth of e-commerce, with limited smartphone penetration and the lack of digital payment systems. There were many fly-by-night operators in India's nascent e-commerce industry. Therefore, consumers predominantly trusted brick-and-mortar retail. Against this backdrop, Flipkart had to overcome multiple challenges to grow.

Therefore, Flipkart's remarkable growth across various dimensions of achievements warrants an in-depth, empirical exploration to understand the broader factors and underlying implications such as:

1. What led to the birth of Flipkart?
2. What was the 'vision and mission' of Flipkart?
3. How did Flipkart deal with its growth challenges in its one and a half decade operations?
4. How did it successfully and sustainably grow the online shopping customer base?
5. Why did it absorb multiple tech start-ups through M&As in its growth process? What has been its success rate?

6. Why did its growth process lead to several tech start-ups from ex-Flipsters?
7. What has contributed to the growth and emergence of Flipkart as the leading e-commerce company in the country today? What role did management and/or ownership play?
8. Did it carry out any innovations on the functional fronts to accelerate its growth?
9. Did it preserve and nurture an entrepreneurial culture among its employees over a period of time?
10. Did it reorganize its business on a regular basis to sustain internal dynamism?
11. How did it respond to the challenges emerging due to the Fourth Industrial Revolution (Industry 4.0)?
12. Did it experience a transition from start-up entrepreneurship to corporate entrepreneurship in the process of growth?

These questions deserve answers as they will have significant policy implications for the promotion of start-up ecosystems and the growth of start-ups in India and elsewhere. Our research attempts to explore answers to the questions raised above, and to derive appropriate policy implications for the stakeholders of start-up ecosystems, including Flipkart itself.

Entrepreneurship, Start-up Dynamics and Growth of Start-ups

Entrepreneurs who create start-ups have a decisive role to play in a dynamic economy (Kritikos, 2014). Start-up entrepreneurs are creators of ideas, jobs and economic value. They create value where none existed before (Thornberry, 2001). They often create new technologies, develop new products or process innovations, and open up new markets. In the process, they contribute immensely to job creation and income generation (Audretsch, 2002). It has been empirically revealed that start-ups show significantly larger rates of average employment growth relative to more matured or established firms (Calvino, et al., 2015).

But the overall contribution of start-ups in any economy would depend on a combination of four elements, namely: (i) the rate of emergence of start-ups, (ii) the average size of start-ups at the time of emergence, (iii) their survival rate, and (iv) the average growth rate of survived start-ups (Calvino, et al., 2015). The emergence, survival and growth of start-ups would depend, on the one hand, on their founders' background, expertise and strategy and that of their employees, and on the other hand, on the strength of the ecosystem surrounding it (Bala Subrahmanya, 2021).

Given these factors, it has been observed empirically that a larger proportion of nascent start-ups fail and exit from the market: globally, 9 out of 10 start-ups fail (Korashev, 2022). While a small proportion do survive, only a minute proportion scales up and grows disproportionately (Bala Subrahmanya, 2022). These are labelled 'high-growth, high-impact firms' and they play a significant role in job creation over time, relative to either well-established firms or smaller start-ups that tend not to grow (Audretsch, 2012; Coad, et al., 2014).

So, what constitutes a 'high-growth, high-impact firm'?

High-growth firms may be defined as the percentage of companies in a population that experience the highest growth, say, the top 1% or 5% of the firms with the highest growth in a year or during a certain number of years (Coad, et al., 2014). Alternatively, they can be defined as firms growing at or above a certain rate for a certain period of years (Fowler and Monteiro, 2018). Among others, the definition offered by OECD is increasingly adapted as the standard in management literature (Audretsch, 2012). The *OECD-Eurostat Manual on Business Demography Statistics* (European Commission, 2007) defines high-growth firms as 'all enterprises with average annualized growth greater than 20% p.a. in revenue as well as employment over a three-year period, and with 10 or more employees at the beginning of the observation period. Growth is thus measured in terms of number of employees and turnover.' Therefore, high-growth firms together can make a big impact on employment and income of a nation. But such high-growth, high-impact firms will not remain start-ups, if they successfully sustain their high growth over a period of time. Therefore, high-growth, high-impact firms need not only be confined to start-ups.

High-Growth, High-Impact Firms: What Determines Their Birth and Growth?

It has been observed in the American context that while a larger proportion of high-growth, high-impact firms are start-ups, the greater impact on employment comes from a few of the largest firms (Audretsch, 2012). The typical high-impact firm is not a start-up, as its mean age is around 25 years old. This suggests that such high-impact firms would have survived their start-up or adolescent phases prior to emerging as high-growth, high-impact firms (Acs, et al., 2008). Or such firms emerged as start-ups but steadily registered high growth over a period of time, transcending their start-up phase, with a consistent contribution to employment and income. This leads to the question: what determines 'high-growth entrepreneurship' particularly in emerging, technology-intensive industries?

The answer lies in the knowledge spillover theory of entrepreneurship. The theory highlights knowledge as an essential source of opportunity and, therefore, entrepreneurial emergence. Knowledge spillovers originate from an initial stock of knowledge that is continuously updated and extended based on experiential learning (Lattacher, et al., 2021). The theory focusses on how new knowledge can influence the cognitive decision-making process inherent in entrepreneurial decision-making to start a new venture (Audretsch, et al., 2006; Acs, et al., 2009).

The basic contention is that entrepreneurship is prompted by the opportunity recognized by newly emerged knowledge, but not adequately exploited through commercialization in the existing organizational context. The application of new knowledge involves uncertainties, asymmetries and high transaction costs. Thus, there would be divergences in the expected value of its applications among those who recognize and perceive that knowledge. Those who appreciate its application value have the incentive to launch a start-up to commercialize the perceived value of their knowledge (Audretsch, 2012). Such start-up entrepreneurship may emerge from both incumbents (established firms) and/or new entrants (entrepreneurs and their organizations) (Acs, et al., 2009). That is, knowledge may spill over from established firms in the form of spinouts (employees-turned-entrepreneurs) or when employees leave to work for other organizations (including direct competitors). Knowledge may also spill through explicit knowledge transfers (such as publications and patents). This is because knowledge is inherently leaky and moves through networks and through stakeholder mobility.

If established firms are efficient in exploiting the knowledge, then there would be fewer opportunities for new entrants. But if existing firms are not adequately or efficiently exploiting the opportunities emerging from new knowledge, it would prompt its exploitation by new entrants through start-ups. This would result in employees leaving a parent firm to join other firms or start their own new ventures, to pursue and exploit knowledge through innovations. Thus, a start-up can be a means for the implementation and commercialization of ideas, and therefore the conduit for the spillover of new knowledge either from an incumbent organization or from a new entrant to a start-up, where it is used for innovative activity and subsequent high growth. But this explains only the birth of entrepreneurship for start-ups in emerging technology industries. What would determine their non-linear growth, particularly in the initial years of their entry into a technology-intensive industry?

The theory of selection (with incomplete information) and evolution of industry propounded by Jovanovic (1982) provides an explanation. A central contention of his theory is that the founder of a new firm does not know what its cost function is, but rather discovers it through the process of learning from the firm's actual post-entry performance. That is, new firm founders would not be certain about the prospects and post-entry performance of their start-ups. Such start-up founders enter an emerging industry with a vague sense of expected post-entry performance but discover their true ability in terms of managerial competence and viability of their start-ups in the market only after their start-ups are established and have started operations. If they discover that their ability and start-up performance exceed expectations, they expand the scale of operations, whereas others who discover their post-entry performance is less than their expectations will contract the scale of operations and even quit the industry (Audretsch, 2012). That is, start-ups learn their efficiency once they enter and start operating in an industry. The efficient ones survive and grow, whereas the inefficient ones decline, fail, and exit (Juvanovic, 1982).

This being the case, what explains the continued above-normal growth of start-ups beyond the 'start-up phase' of their lifecycle in the long run? This assumes significance because with growth a large company tends to lose dynamism and develops inertia, risk aversion and complacency, and thereby loses the rigour of growth (Thornberry, 2001). It leads to the question: how can established organizations sustain entrepreneurial zeal, innovation and competitiveness on a long-term basis?

Corporate entrepreneurship provides the answer. Recognized as a potentially viable means for nurturing innovation and sustaining corporate competitiveness (Covin and Miles,

1999), corporate entrepreneurship involves teams within a firm, led by intrapreneurs who promote entrepreneurial behavior within large enterprises, proactively engaging in risky projects so that they lead to innovative products and services, as well as new organizational procedures resulting in organizational renewal and growth (Thomson and McNamara, 2001).

Corporate entrepreneurship refers to entrepreneurial activities such as innovation, new venturing and organizational renewal within established organizations (Zahra, 1996). Thus, it is typically associated with large public firms, though it would vary from one firm to another in its composition, practice and outcomes. Corporate entrepreneurship has been increasingly adopted and practised by established organizations as a means of sustaining their competitive advantage with innovativeness, courage, risk propensity, and entrepreneurial leadership (Kuratko, 2009). Among others, it would involve M&As of new, young firms (King, et al., 2018).

The above discussion throws light on the birth and growth of firms in the context of a technology-intensive industry. The discussion is summarized and presented in Figure 1.1. It is the 'knowledge spillover' that leads to the creation of a start-up in a technology-intensive industry, whereas it is the 'superior efficiency' realized by the start-up founder/s after the entry of the start-up which would spur its growth beyond the 'start-up phase'. The adoption of 'corporate entrepreneurship strategy' would enable the sustenance of its competitiveness for its long-term growth. This would broadly explain the birth and growth of high-growth, high-impact firms in a technology-intensive industry.

It is against this backdrop that we have attempted to explore and analyse the birth and growth of Flipkart, which emerged as a tech start-up in 2007 and has grown to become one of the largest e-commerce companies in India since then (Dalal, 2019, Walmart Press Release, 2018). As per the initial definition of a 'start-up' promulgated by the Government of India (Department of Industrial Policy and Promotion, 2016), Flipkart ceased to be a start-up when it completed five years of operations. The age of an entity to be recognized as a start-up has been revised upwards since then. According to the current definition, a start-up is an entity that is not more than 10 years from the start of operations (Startupindia, 2022a). Thus, Flipkart's impressive annual growth transcended its start-up phase to enable it to emerge as one of India's leading e-commerce companies.

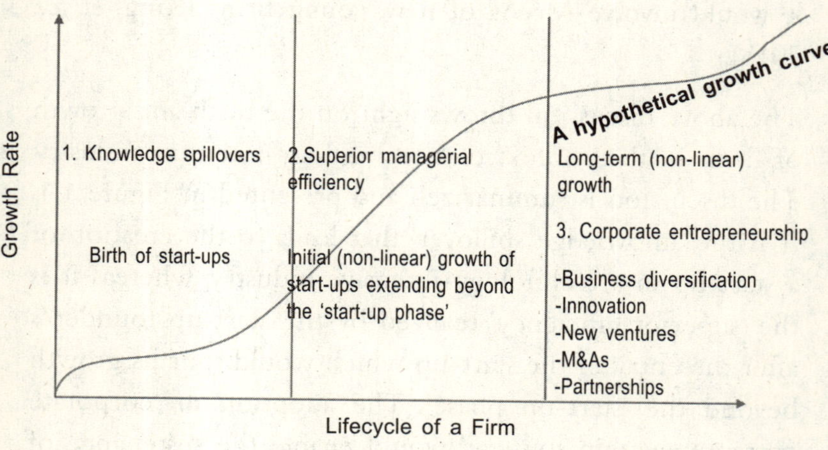

Figure 1.1: Birth and growth of 'high-growth, high-impact firms' in a technology-intensive industry

While the Flipkart founders' 'knowledge spillover' and 'superior efficiency' may have played a decisive role in its emergence as a start-up and subsequent growth, its long-run growth and current contributions deserve a critical examination. Our preliminary enquiries and exploration enabled us to conclude that pursuing 'corporate entrepreneurship' played a significant role in the growth of Flipkart. Therefore, our research objectives, scope and methods of analysis are designed to analyse this concept in detail.

Research Objectives

The key research objectives are as follows:

1. To explore the origin, growth and ecosystem contributions of Flipkart and its determinants, in the context of corporate entrepreneurship
2. To examine the key characteristics of entrepreneurial culture (as part of corporate entrepreneurship strategy) as they prevail in Flipkart today
3. To ascertain the determinants of current level of corporate entrepreneurship in Flipkart
4. To derive managerial and policy implications from the corporate entrepreneurship strategy and growth experience of Flipkart

Scope of the Study and Background

The study is confined to Flipkart, its corporate entrepreneurship strategy and growth since inception.

Flipkart's growth has seen multiple achievements, not only related to job creation and income generation, but more importantly boosting India's start-up ecosystem in general and that of Bangalore in particular. Table 1.1 summarizes Flipkart's achievements over the recent past.

Table 1.1
Status and Dimensions of Flipkart Achievements (as of 2021–22)

Status & Dimensions of Achievements	Number/Value
Valuation	
2021	US$37.6 billion
Market Coverage	
Number of registered sellers	>14 lakh
Number of registered customer base	~500 million
Number of product offerings	>150 million
Number of product categories	>80
Number of cities/towns covered	100% serviceable pin codes in India
Employment (Human Resource) Generation	
Number of employees—full-time	~15,000
Start-up Ecosystem Contributions	
Number of ex-Flipkart employees who turned entrepreneurs	>200
Number of start-ups founded by ex-employees	>200
Number of start-ups backed by Flipkart, Flipkart founders, and/or current and ex-employees	Many
Number of start-ups acquired or acquihired	22

Equity-based investments in start-ups through Flipkart Leap Ahead (FLA) program
Meeting the dynamic needs of start-ups across different lifecycle stages through Flipkart Innovation Network (FLIN) program

Source: Multiple published sources (Employment: NDTV Profit, PTI (2023), Business Standard *New Delhi (2023);* ***Market Coverage:*** *Flipkart Brands;* ***Startup Ecosystem Contribution:*** *GOVINDAYAPALLI-thestrategystory, 2020)*

Since its birth as an online book store in 2007, Flipkart has grown to become a pan-Indian brand in a matter of a decade and a half. In July 2021, Flipkart's valuation exceeded US$37 billion (Walmart Press Release, 2021); its revenue in 2022 was INR 51,176 crore/US$ 6.52 billion (*Onmanorama*). These are broad indicators of its financial performance, as reflected in the market coverage Flipkart attained over the period. In the process, Flipkart emerged as a major link between domestic producers, domestic sellers and domestic customers, generating direct employment for approximately 20,000 staff who form the talent base of the company. This sums up Flipkart's economic contributions.

However, Flipkart's contribution extends beyond economic performance. Its contribution to the start-up ecosystem is equally noteworthy. Till date, more than 200 Flipkart employees have become entrepreneurs, founding their own start-ups after leaving Flipkart. A majority of the more than 200 start-ups created by these former employees are in Bangalore. In addition, Flipkart founders and its current and former employees have supported several start-ups as sources of finance, mentorship, human resources and market penetration, among others.

Furthermore, some start-ups founded by ex-Flipsters failed and exited from the market, and subsequently, some of these founders re-joined Flipkart as employees. Some others joined other start-ups or large companies as employees. Till date, Flipkart has acquired 22 start-ups, helping it diversify and recruit talent—with an average of 1.5 start-ups acquired every year since its founding (Rath - Startup Talky, 2022). In recent times, Flipkart has promoted start-ups directly in two ways: through direct equity investments and by assisting the dynamic needs of start-ups across their lifecycle, leading to their accelerated growth. Flipkart has thus emerged as the 'leading contributor' to 'entrepreneurship nurturing' for the promotion of start-ups in India.

As one of the earliest start-ups to become a unicorn and one of the largest e-commerce companies in India, Flipkart has been a major contributor to the start-up ecosystem of the country. There are several key lessons to learn from it for prospective start-up founders, founders of start-ups operating in different stages of their lifecycles, and stakeholders of the start-up ecosystem. Therefore, Flipkart is chosen for a detailed case study.

Sources of Data and Methods of Analysis

We have used both secondary and primary data for the analysis of the first three research objectives. The first research objective has been analysed based on secondary data on Flipkart available in the public domain, including media reports. The information has been picked up from media reports including Flipkart's press releases. We developed a chronology of events (from October 2007 till April 2022) describing the major developments that contributed to the growth of the company. Based on these descriptions, we have derived inferences to develop 'a model of corporate entrepreneurship' that emerged from Flipkart.

The second and third research objectives have been analysed based on primary data gathered from: (i) personal interviews and (ii) questionnaire-based survey, respectively. The primary data gathered from personal interviews are used to analyse the second research objective, whereas primary data gathered through circulation of a questionnaire are used to analyse the third research objective. For both personal interviews and questionnaire circulation, we have selected respondents on a judgement basis. That is, judgemental or purposive sampling is adopted for the study.

Therefore, a description on judgement or purposive sampling is in order. It is a non-probability sampling technique in which particular respondents are chosen to provide information that cannot be obtained from other forms of sampling (Maxwell, 1996). Here, respondents are chosen based on the judgement of the researchers because they believe that they can obtain a representative sample by using their sound judgement. Particularly, the use of judgemental sampling is considered appropriate in three situations: firstly, to select unique respondents who are especially informative; secondly, to select members of a difficult-to-reach, specialized population; and thirdly, to identify particular types of respondents for an in-depth investigation. Purposive sampling is widely used in qualitative research as a means of identifying and selecting 'information-rich' cases related to the phenomenon of interest (Palinkas, et al., 2015).

Since the proposed study is an exclusive case study focussing on the growth and contributions of Flipkart over time, we concluded that we need to interact with those who are adequately knowledgeable on the company and its related developments. Accordingly, we decided to identify respondents ourselves for personal interviews, followed by circulation of a questionnaire for a survey. Thus, this research is exclusively based on surveys conducted within Flipkart and the people we interviewed, including Flipsters and Flipsters-turned-entrepreneurs.

The purpose of holding personal interviews is to understand the decisive characteristics of the 'entrepreneurial culture' prevailing in Flipkart, for the analysis of the second research objective. To do this, we identified five categories of respondents, namely, the current CEO Kalyan Krishnamurthy, one of the co-founders/former director Binny Bansal, tenured senior executives including two intrapreneurs, founders of start-ups acquired by Flipkart, and founders of start-ups created by ex-Flipkart employees (ex-Flipsters). The criteria adopted for selection of the five categories of respondents are given in Annexure 2.

We designed separate interview protocols for each of the five categories with an exclusive thrust on strategic renewal (organizational restructuring), innovation, and entrepreneurship support that has been undertaken or provided within the company. The personal interviews, based on an interview protocol, were conducted online from October 2021 to April 2022. Each interview took about one hour. Both the research investigators took down notes as the respondents replied to each of the listed questions.

Table 1.2
Respondents for Personal Interviews (as of 2022)

Category	Number of Respondents
Current CEO of Flipkart	1
Co-founder/Director	1
Tenured executives (including two intrapreneurs)	15
Founders of acquired start-ups	6
Founders of start-ups created by ex-Flipsters	22
Total	45

These five categories have been subsequently classified into three groups: namely, CEO and co-founder/director; senior executives (including intrapreneurs) and founders of start-ups acquired by Flipkart through M&As; and ex-Flipster founders of start-ups. While the CEO and the co-founder represented ownership and management, tenured executives and founders of acquired start-ups who are currently Flipkart employees together represented top management involved in decision-making and/or implementation. The ex-Flipsters who are founders of start-ups, operating outside of Flipkart, represented former employees of Flipkart. These ex-Flipsters had served Flipkart for a minimum of three years to a maximum of seven years. Personal interviews with three different groups of stakeholders of Flipkart enabled us to elicit multiple perspectives of the entrepreneurial culture prevalent in Flipkart. The primary data gathered through personal interviews formed the basis for qualitative analysis of the second research objective.

Thus, we adopted the triangulation of three different data sources to understand the presence and characteristics of entrepreneurial culture at Flipkart.

The term 'triangulation' refers to the practice of using multiple sources of data or multiple approaches to analyse data to enhance the credibility of a research study (Salkind, 2010). It is used for three main purposes: to enhance validity, to develop a comprehensive picture of a research problem, and to explore different ways of understanding a research question (Nightingale, 2020). Most often, triangulation helps validate research findings by checking that different methods or different observers of the same phenomenon produce the same results. Thus, it is the convergence emerging out of two or more sources of data that enhances the credibility of findings derived from qualitative analysis.

The third research objective has been analysed quantitatively, based on primary data obtained by e-mailing a questionnaire to a select group of 50 managerial executives in Flipkart. The objective of the questionnaire was to elicit information on factors that contribute to or determine the level of corporate entrepreneurship prevalent in Flipkart. For this purpose, we used the Corporate Entrepreneurship Assessment Instrument (CEAI) developed and validated by Kuratko, et al. (2014). Further, we ascertained the nature of resource authority and organizational ownership at Flipkart, by making use of the four models of corporate entrepreneurship developed by

Wolcott and Lippitz (2007). Additionally, the background characteristics of 50 management executives (including whether they are proactive, motivated, risk-taker and entrepreneurial) are obtained.

Table 1.3 presents the broad composition of respondents approached for the questionnaire, for gathering primary data. These Flipkart employees are chosen from different verticals, different levels of hierarchy, and different genders to ensure approximate representation. Their experience varied from a minimum of three years to a maximum of 12 years. About 75% of them are male and the rest are female. In terms of hierarchy, about 13% are in junior management, 67% in middle management, and 20% in senior management. Only those who have worked at Flipkart for a minimum of three years are chosen, to ensure respondents are fairly knowledgeable and familiar with Flipkart operations.

The CEAI instrument-based data enabled us to arrive at the level of corporate entrepreneurship prevalent in Flipkart. The nature of organizational ownership revealed the kind of support provided to corporate entrepreneurship by the management. The individual characteristics of respondents represented talent of managerial executives, acquired and nurtured. These variables enabled us to quantitatively ascertain the determining influence of ownership (top management) and talent on the prevailing corporate entrepreneurship in Flipkart.

Table 1.3
Respondents for Questionnaire-based Survey

Category/Group	Number of Respondents
Business functions	15
Corporate functions	15
Technology functions	15
Supply chain management functions	5
Total	50

We carried out stepwise multiple regression analysis for the following equation:

CE = f (C + O) where CE = corporate entrepreneurship, C = characteristics of management executives, and O = nature of organizational ownership

We tested the following hypotheses: H0: Individual characteristics of managerial executives and/or nature of organizational ownership will not have a determining influence on the level of corporate entrepreneurship at Flipkart.

HA: Individual characteristics of managerial executives and/or nature of organizational ownership will have a determining influence on the level of corporate entrepreneurship at Flipkart.

A Summary of the Research Process of the Study

The research process followed for the study is succinctly presented in Figure 1.2. This is an exploratory study to ascertain the nature of the corporate entrepreneurship strategy pursued by Flipkart and its outcomes. At the outset, we tentatively defined the research problem, focussing on Flipkart. This was followed by a detailed literature survey. As we progressed with reviewing relevant literature, we refined the research problem. Subsequently, we identified five categories of respondents for personal interviews. Accordingly, we prepared five different interview protocols. As we progressed with the personal interviews conducted online with respondents, we simultaneously prepared the questionnaire for circulation among a select group of managerial executives, not covered in the personal interviews. We circulated the questionnaire among the chosen managerial executives for gathering primary data.

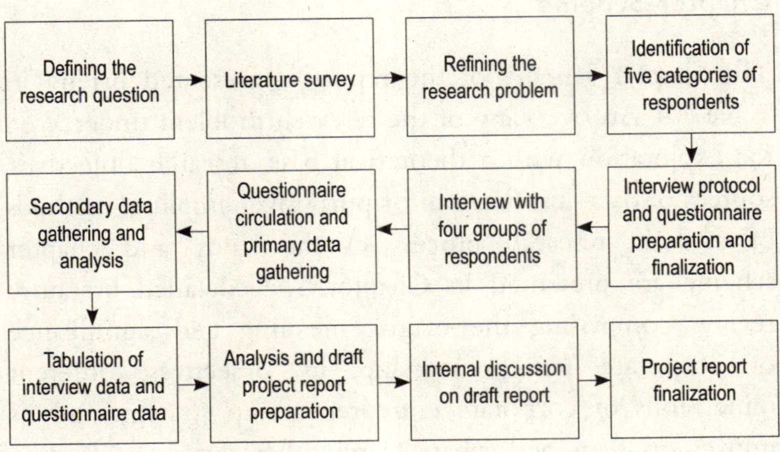

Figure 1.2: Research process

Based on personal interviews and primary data, we decided to gather secondary data concerning all the major developments relating to Flipkart. Accordingly, we gathered secondary data through various sources of print/online media relating to Flipkart, since its inception till 2022. We did a qualitative analysis of secondary data leading to the development of a corporate entrepreneurship model that emerged from Flipkart. Subsequently, we tabulated the data obtained from personal interviews leading to data triangulation, based on which we analysed the characteristics of the entrepreneurial culture at Flipkart. Thereafter, based on primary data analysis, we ascertained the level of corporate entrepreneurship at Flipkart and its determinants. With the overall analyses, we prepared the draft report, held internal discussions on the draft, leading to its finalization.

Chapter Scheme

The chapter scheme of the report is presented briefly in Table 1.4. An overview of the research problem undertaken for exploration with a theoretical base, research objectives, sources of data, justification for purposive sampling, methods of analysis, research process of the study and chapter scheme are presented in Chapter 1. A detailed literature review comprising the origin, meaning and significance of corporate entrepreneurship, its objectives, different dimensions of corporate entrepreneurship strategy, and its impact on firm performance and other outcomes leading to the identification of research gaps, and formulation of a conceptual model of corporate entrepreneurship linking its determinants, process and outcomes are presented in Chapter 2.

Table 1.4
Chapter Scheme of the Report

Chapter No.	Focus	Contents
1	Introduction	Basic concepts, theoretical base, research objectives, scope, data sources, methods of analysis, research process and chapter scheme
2	Literature review	Origin, meaning and significance of corporate entrepreneurship, its objectives, dimensions of strategy, outcomes, research gaps and formulation of a conceptual framework
3	Growth of Flipkart since inception till 2022	Description of the chronology of events leading to the growth of Flipkart, key growth parameters, analysis of the evolution of corporate entrepreneurship strategy, and formulation of a model
4	Entrepreneurial culture	Analysis based on data triangulation w.r.t. characteristics of entrepreneurial culture prevailing in Flipkart and its implications
5	Level of corporate entrepreneurship and its determinants	Quantitative analysis-based estimation of the level of corporate entrepreneurship and its determinants

Chapter No.	Focus	Contents
6	Summary and conclusions	Summary of the study, its key findings, inferences, implications for Flipkart and the ecosystem, and scope for future research

Chapter 3 includes a chronology of events describing all the major developments concerning Flipkart under two broad phases of its growth: from 2007 until August 2018, when Walmart invested in Flipkart, and then from August 2018 till April 2022, covering its growth achievements in terms of revenue and employment. The chapter features an in-depth analysis of the corporate entrepreneurship strategy pursued by Flipkart since inception and the corporate entrepreneurship model that emerged from Flipkart.

In Chapter 4, the entrepreneurial culture and its key characteristics are ascertained and discussed based on data triangulation (from three different groups of stakeholders of Flipkart).

The background characteristics of respondents, the kind of managerial support respondents perceived they received for corporate entrepreneurship at Flipkart, the level of corporate entrepreneurship at Flipkart and its determinants are analysed and presented in Chapter 5.

The summary and conclusions of the overall study, its managerial and policy implications, and limitations of the study are described in Chapter 6.

Annexure 1.1

Unicorns in India: A Note

A unicorn refers to a start-up that is a privately held company with a value of US$1 billion or more. The term 'unicorn' was first used by Aileen Lee, founder of Cowboy Ventures, in 2013 with reference to 39 start-ups that had a valuation of more than US$1 billion each (Paytm for Business, 2022). There are certain unique features that are associated with unicorns. They are, in general, tech-savvy, pioneers in their niche, privately owned, and growth-driven, and carry out disruptive innovations for consumers (Paytm for Business, 2022). Another unique feature of these unicorns is that they regularly resort to M&As as a growth strategy (*India Briefing*, 2022).

Similar to the overall start-up ecosystem, India accounts for the third largest share of unicorns globally today after the US and China (Invest India, 2022). Inmobi was India's first unicorn that emerged in 2011. Flipkart emerged as one of the early unicorns in India in 2012. In 2021, India accounted for its hundredth unicorn (*India Briefing*, 2022). Thus, in about a decade, along with the rapid emergence and growth of start-ups, the number of unicorns has also increased considerably, indicating the growth and maturing of the Indian start-up ecosystem. In fact, the number of unicorns emerging in India has rapidly increased since 2018. More than two-thirds of the present unicorns have emerged over 2020 to 2022 (Table 1).

Number of Unicorns in India

Year	Number of Start-ups Achieving Unicorn Status	
	Absolute	Cumulative
2011–15	8	8
2016	5	13
2017	1	14
2018	10	24
2019	7	31
2020	11	42
2021	44	86
2022 (till July)	17	103
Total	103	103

In terms of geographical spread, Bangalore accounts for the highest share of unicorns followed by NCR Delhi and Mumbai. A majority of the unicorns are located in the five major start-up hubs, namely Bangalore, NCR Delhi, Mumbai, Pune and Chennai (*Venture Intelligence*, 2021). These unicorns are spread across a variety of sectors such as e-commerce, fintech, agritech, logistics, edutech, AI, biotech, media and entertainment, gaming, fitness, SaaS, health tech, retail tech, electric vehicle, aerospace, social media, and food and beverages, amongst others. Thus, the growth of start-ups in India has spread across regions as well as sectors.

Three further developments with respect to unicorns are noteworthy:

1. Some of the unicorns have gone public and have thus become publicly listed companies.

2. Some of the unicorns have scaled up and become 'decacorns' (a valuation of more than US$10 billion) in the process. Flipkart, Nykaa and Swiggy are the current decacorns in India. (Invest India, 2022, *Moneycontrol*, Crunchbase, 2021)
3. Some of the start-ups have lost their unicorn status due to a valuation degrading event or due to shutdown of operations.

Thus, the growth of start-ups has a non-linear and tumultuous path. It can lead to acquiring unicorn status and further growth towards a decacorn status, and/or attract M&A by other well-established large companies, or lose steam and thereby lose the unicorn status, and even exit from the market.

Annexure 1.2

Criteria for Selection of Respondents for Personal Interviews (as of 2022)

Group	Category of Respondents	Justification for Inclusion
1	CEO: Kalyan Krishnamurthy	CEO of Flipkart and key member in nurturing the entrepreneurial culture in Flipkart
	Co-founder/ Director: Binny Bansal	Co-founder of Flipkart; founded the entrepreneurial mindset in the ethos of Flipkart
2	13 tenured executives	Chosen tenured employees who have demonstrated the culture of entrepreneurship in their respective organizations. We took a 1) Gender split of 30F: 70M 2) Business units (BU) split: Biz: 4, Tech: 4, Corp: 4, SCM: 1; or BU split: Biz: 31%, Tech: 31%, Corp: 31%, SCM: 7% 3) Tenure split: approximately 40%: 7–8 years, 30%: 9–10 years, and 30%: 11–13 years

Group	Category of Respondents	Justification for Inclusion
	2 intrapreneurs	These individuals have been true entrepreneurs within Flipkart and have owned many projects and initiatives that needed to be scaled up from 0 to 1
	6 founders of start-ups acquired by Flipkart	We believe that start-up founders bring in a lot of innovation We took a split of respondents as below: BU split: Biz: 50%, Tech: 50%
3	22 founders of start-ups by ex-Flipsters	These are employees who moved out of Flipkart to start their own entrepreneurial journeys. The only criterion here was that they left Flipkart to begin their start-up journeys

2

Objectives, Strategy and Outcomes of Corporate Entrepreneurship: Literature Review

Introduction

The emergence, growth and exit of firms from the market is a common phenomenon observed in almost every economy, irrespective of the stage of development. This is applicable to firms of different sizes—be they new ventures, or micro, small, medium or large firms, including MNCs. This is because firms of different sizes perennially face threats, pressure and challenges of various kinds (Nason, et al., 2015). Given this, those that survive and succeed face the threat of competition increasingly as they grow over time.

In fact, surviving and maintaining the growth trend becomes increasingly challenging for firms as they operate in an increasingly competitive business environment, particularly in the globalization era since the 1990s (Paunivic and Dima, 2014). Moreover, rapid technological changes have put added pressure on the management of firms (Tribbitt, 2017). This is particularly true for those that have grown over time and become large. In other words, sustaining or accelerating growth is a relatively greater challenge for large established firms than smaller firms.

Large firms growing in size develop a hierarchy for their employees, set rules and regulations for them to follow, along with targets to achieve. This results in the emergence of an internal bureaucratic structure. As a result, the organization becomes rigid and inflexible. Bureaucratic procedures and structures that emerge during the process of growth stifle or gradually impede dynamism, innovation and ultimately growth itself (Zimmerman, 2010). In the process, the organization develops resistance to change and loses its entrepreneurial spirit.

In other words, as companies grow, they develop structures and systems to control, gradually increasing complexity, and as a result, it becomes increasingly difficult to propose and implement changes (Schaeffer, 2015). The increased size and complexity, the systems, the processes and procedures result in structural inertia and growing resistance to change (Scheferrer, 2013).

Thus, preserving the entrepreneurial spirit becomes a challenge as the organization grows in size and age (Dutta, 2018), and its ability to expand further may eventually diminish (Burgelman, 1984). To overcome the challenges to growth, a firm must achieve a sustainable competitive advantage (Tribbitt, 2017). This necessitates a large and growing firm to develop dynamism, flexibility, adaptability, responsiveness and innovativeness (Paunovic and Dima, 2014). For any organization to sustain its competitive advantage, it must engage in some form of entrepreneurship so as to continuously compete in the marketplace and steadily increase its stakeholder value (Zimmerman, 2010). In mature markets, it is believed that a firm is bound to fail if it does not have the ability to engage in some level of corporate entrepreneurship (Turro, et al., 2014).

An entrepreneurial spirit and innovative climate need to be nurtured constantly from the top management till the bottom, involving every individual employee at the operational levels (Paunovic and Dima, 2014). Empirical researchers have repeatedly highlighted that corporate entrepreneurship can be adopted to improve competitive positioning and transform large companies and their markets, as opportunities for value-creating innovation are developed and exploited (Covin and Miles, 1999). Corporate entrepreneurship is a term used to describe entrepreneurial behaviour inside established large organizations (Kuratko and Morris, 2018; Burns, 2008). Thus, the term 'corporate entrepreneurship' is typically associated with large public firms (Nason, et al., 2015). Against this backdrop, it is appropriate to know the origin, significance and meaning of the corporate entrepreneurship concept.

Corporate Entrepreneurship: Origin, Meaning and Significance

Corporate entrepreneurship has evolved as an important strategy in organizational development over a period of more than five decades, from the early 1970s (Turro, et al., 2014; Kuratko, et al., 2015). It is considered to be the most effective method to achieve high levels of organizational performance and, therefore, an important potential growth strategy (Kuratko and Audretsch, 2013). It is a potentially viable means of enhancing and sustaining corporate competitiveness (Covin and Miles, 1999) and an instrument for corporate enterprises to distinguish themselves from others, to create sustainable competitive advantage (Tribbitt, 2017). Irrespective of its objectives, corporate entrepreneurship has rapidly spread to embrace all types of established organizations, though the term 'corporate entrepreneurship' itself is normally associated with large public firms (Nason, et al., 2015; Narayanan, et al., 2009; Morris, et al., 2011).

Used to describe the prevalence and occurrence of entrepreneurship in large-sized companies (Morris, et al., 2008), corporate entrepreneurship is continued entrepreneurship in large organizations (Sakhdari, 2016). Its significance lies in the fact that it enables corporate vitality and wealth generation on a sustained basis in the ever-competitive global economy (Dess, et al., 2003). The pursuance of corporate entrepreneurship enables large firms to be entrepreneurial on a continuous basis over their lifecycle and stay ahead of their rivals (Dutta, 2018). Corporate entrepreneurship as a concept has evolved over time and, therefore, it is defined in different ways at different points of time (Kuratko and Audretsch, 2013). In the process, the recognized scope of corporate entrepreneurship has undergone revision as well as expansion (Corbett, et al., 2013). However, since the 1990s, business researchers have started converging on the meaning and contents of corporate entrepreneurship.

Corporate entrepreneurship takes place within established organizations comprising creation of new businesses, strategic renewal, or innovation (Zahra and Covin, 1995; Zahra, 1996; Sharma and Chrisman, 1999). According to Thornsby (2001), corporate entrepreneurship has three dimensions, namely innovation, corporate venturing, and strategic renewal. Dess, et al. (2003), further stress on the key components of corporate entrepreneurship to comprise organizational renewal, innovation, and establishing new ventures. This has been supported by Hayton and Kelley (2006) when they stated that corporate entrepreneurship would involve a diverse set of activities such as innovations, internal and external corporate ventures, and the development of new business models, leading to the discovery and pursuit of new business opportunities. However, firms vary in their ability to nurture corporate entrepreneurship and exploit new business opportunities due to differences in firm size, external environment, organizational vision, culture, and structure.

Broadly, corporate entrepreneurship refers to the development of new businesses within large and established organizations (Birkinshaw, 2003). According to Ireland, et al. (2006, p. 10), corporate entrepreneurship is 'a process through which individuals in an established firm pursue entrepreneurial opportunities to innovate without regard to the level and nature of currently available resources.' Corporate entrepreneurship constitutes organizational renewal involving innovation and venturing, leading to new products, processes and even technologies (Zimmerman, 2010). Corporate entrepreneurship is a multidimensional construct and it has been defined as the summation of organization renewal, innovation and venturing efforts undertaken within a corporate enterprise (Turro, et al., 2014). According to Bierwerth, et al. (2015), corporate entrepreneurship is an activity which focusses on identifying and exploiting new business opportunities by means of strategic renewal, innovation and corporate venturing.

Bouchard and Fayolle (2018) present that corporate entrepreneurship refers to the development of new businesses within established firms, and it involves internal teams and leverages internal resources of a firm. They contend that corporate entrepreneurship can be either a spontaneous or a management- induced process. Spontaneous corporate entrepreneurship owes its emergence to unplanned process triggered by employees who engage spontaneously in the development of a new activity within an established firm using the available resources of a firm. This is a bottom-up process. On the contrary, induced corporate entrepreneurship owes its origin to management practices that a firm adopts consciously to encourage and support the development of new activities by employees and the outcomes of these practices (Bouchard and Fayolle, 2018). This is a top-down approach.

Thus, in the last three decades since the mid-1990s, there has been a greater convergence among business researchers on what constitutes corporate entrepreneurship. Though different scholars have categorized the domain of corporate entrepreneurship in different ways (Bouchard and Fayolle, 2018; Hisrich and Kearney, 2012), broadly they are confined to innovation, venturing and strategic renewal within existing firms (Sakhdari, 2018). Given the conceptual understanding of corporate entrepreneurship, it is necessary to ascertain its key objectives.

Corporate Entrepreneurship: Objectives

Corporate entrepreneurship is undertaken to deal with multiple issues, such as a stagnation of sales emerging from a lack of innovation, shortcomings in existing management methods, and the attrition of talented and innovative employees out of frustration caused by bureaucratic procedures and structure prevalent in the company (Kuratko, et al., 1990). Corporate entrepreneurship is considered an important remedy for a lack of innovative and competitive capabilities within organizations (Turro, et al., 2014). It is a means of acquiring sustainable competitive advantage with innovativeness, risk propensity, and entrepreneurial leadership for a firm in response to competition emerging from start-ups as well as other established firms (Glinyanova, et al., 2021). It is a means of achieving business development and growth in revenue and profits (Davidsson, 2015).

Generally, firms that exhibit corporate entrepreneurship are considered dynamic, flexible entities that challenge the status quo and usurp any new business opportunity when it arises (Kuratko, et al., 2012). According to Miles and Covin (2002), corporate entrepreneurship strategy is adopted by firms to achieve three main objectives: namely, to build an innovative capability in such a way that the firm becomes more entrepreneurial and offers no resistance but rather embraces change, to enable the firm to understand entrepreneurial opportunities and proactively diversify into new areas, and to steadily achieve higher financial returns. But according to Bouchard and Fayolle (2018), firms foster corporate entrepreneurship to revitalize the organization, to increase agility, to better capitalize on intangible assets, and to penetrate the international market.

Corporate entrepreneurship has emerged in established organizations for a variety of reasons such as profitability, strategic renewal, innovativeness, knowledge generation for developing future revenue streams and for an effective configuration of resources to acquire competitive advantages (Kuratko, et al., 2015). The ultimate objective of pursuing corporate entrepreneurship by a large organization is to achieve higher levels of corporate performance, growth and profitability (Sakhdari, 2018). Accordingly, Shane and Venkataraman (2000) have contended that the presence of corporate entrepreneurship strategy implies a firm's strategic intent to continuously and deliberately leverage entrepreneurial opportunities for growth. A corporate entrepreneurship strategy is based on a firm's vision to rely on entrepreneurial behaviour that intentionally rejuvenates an organization and determines the scope of its operations through recognition of entrepreneurial opportunities for exploitation on a perennial basis (Ireland, et al., 2009).

In the process, the firm can achieve higher levels of corporate performance, growth and profitability (Sakhdari, 2016).

Overall, there is greater unanimity among business researchers as far as the objective of corporate entrepreneurship is concerned: it is adopted to steadily improve a firm's performance, which can have two major dimensions: objective and subjective. Objective firm performance would include financial performance comprising return on sales (RoS), return on assets (RoA), and profitability (Zahra, et al., 2000). It may even include sales growth and market share, growth in investment and employment, and the attrition rate of employees.

On the other hand, subjective performance would refer to non-financial performance such as customer satisfaction or perceived financial performance, such as perceived profitability of a firm relative to its competitors (Bierwerth, et al., 2015). It can further include how attractive the firm is to employees and prospective employees, investors' impressions of the firm, and its public image, among others. By and large, it would be justifiable to state that a large firm would focus more on steadily improving objective firm performance rather than on subjective firm performance. It may be appropriate to argue that objective firm performance would influence subjective performance, sooner or later. Given this understanding, it is pertinent to explore the different dimensions of corporate entrepreneurship strategy adopted for its implementation.

Corporate Entrepreneurship: Strategy Dimensions

Corporate entrepreneurship in general is manifested in multiple ways including new venture creation, setting up new autonomous units within and/or outside the company, mergers and acquisitions, innovation, pro-actively reorganizing the structure of the company, etc. (Gautam and Verma, 1997). According to Turro, et al. (2015), a corporate entrepreneurial firm is one that is engaged in product-market innovations, undertakes risky innovations, often comes up with proactive innovations, and thus keeps itself ahead of its competitors.

Firms pursuing corporate entrepreneurship strategy continuously explore new businesses as well as new ways of carrying business within their existing domains (Kuratko, et al., 2014). The former necessitates innovations whereas the latter would require business reorganization or even business diversification. According to Buchard and Fayolle (2018), corporate entrepreneurship is a dual process. Firstly, a business idea is progressively transformed from a concept to a prototype and further to a minimum viable product, leading to a business activity that is scaled up steadily into an established business. Secondly, it is an organizational process through which the launched business gains legitimacy, acquires new resources internally, and establishes strategic and structural ties with the rest of the organization.

Guth and Ginsberg (1990) identified two categories of corporate entrepreneurship activities, namely, business venturing and strategic renewal. Business venturing refers to the creation of new ventures within existing organizations, whereas strategic renewal refers to the transformation of organizations through renewal of the key ideas on which they are built. But business venturing need not be confined to only within the organization. In this regard, some scholars differentiate between internal and external corporate venturing.

In internal corporate venturing, new ventures emerge and operate within the firm, yet they may act as semi-autonomous entities (Morris, et al., 2010). External corporate venturing refers to the creation of new ventures outside the firm in which the firm leverages external partners in an equity or non-equity relationship (Schildt, et al., 2005). In addition, a firm may use other governance modes such as joint ventures, non-equity alliance, and acquisitions of failed/successful start-ups, among others. This is substantiated by Kuratko, et al. (2015), who distinguished between two different dimensions of corporate venturing: internal for any innovation created by a firm and external for innovation that is created outside the firm. Internal corporate venturing leads to the creation of new businesses which operate within the corporate structure of the firm. In contrast, external corporate venturing involves new business ventures created by outsiders in which the firm may invest and which it may later acquire.

In addition, a company may go for strategic alliances with other firms which have complementary business interests and resources. A firm pursuing corporate entrepreneurship is most likely to experience resource/talent gaps. In such circumstances, it would explore opportunities for collaboration with external firms which have complementary skills and resources, among others, to overcome resource gaps (Teng,

2007). Alternatively, it may explicitly acquire other start-ups that have the potential to grow big in the business verticals where the firm wants to diversify (Teng, 2007). In fact, M&As are another way for entrepreneurial firms to acquire strategic assets to achieve the objectives of corporate entrepreneurship (Farinos, et.al., 2011).

According to Dess, et al. (2003), corporate entrepreneurship strategy implementation involves accumulating, converting and leveraging resources for gaining a competitive edge in the form of developing product, process and administrative innovations to rejuvenate and redefine the firm and its markets and industries. A fundamental requirement for achieving these objectives is constant organizational learning. Organizational learning is a process that depends on individual employee characteristics and contributions. Given this, employees in an organization are supposed to have the required competencies to integrate existing and new knowledge which would enable them to recognize, evaluate and exploit entrepreneurial opportunities through innovations. Individual competencies represent a combination of knowledge, skills and personality characteristics such as being a team player, a boundary spanner, or simply a leader (Hayton and Kelley, 2006).

Promoting organizational learning processes among employees to strengthen their ability to analyse markets and formulate new products is a significant characteristic of corporate entrepreneurial behaviour in a firm (Zahra, 2015). To encourage the adoption of corporate entrepreneurial behaviour among employees, a large firm must develop a system of positive enforcement, form

Innovation Teams (I-Teams), support and encourage an entrepreneurial environment, provide intra-capital for corporate entrepreneurs, reduce organizational boundaries, and facilitate top management support (Tseng and Tseng, 2019).

For this, there is a constant need to nurture an entrepreneurial spirit and innovative climate through the hierarchy, from top management down to each individual employee at the operational levels. To achieve this, it is essential to encourage employees who reactively or proactively demonstrate entrepreneurship and initiative in implementing new business ventures. Promoting an entrepreneurial culture among employees has a profound influence on corporate entrepreneurship within a firm (Turro, et al., 2014). Such firms stand to gain in the long run (Paunovic and Dima, 2014). Thus, corporate entrepreneurship is firmly embedded within a firm's human capital. It is the human capital within the process of corporate entrepreneurship which achieves, sustains and/or develops competitive advantage for a firm (Corbett, et al., 2013).

In fact, employees play a unique role in promoting corporate entrepreneurship. They are an important source for companies to achieve their vision and mission. Individual employees help firms to absorb and deploy knowledge, enabling the development of competitive advantages. Towards this end, employers must empower employees to act entrepreneurially by cultivating an entrepreneurial culture, including entrepreneurial orientation. When employees are empowered within their firm, they experience increased motivation (Tribbitt, 2017).

When employees are offered opportunities to conceive, develop and implement an idea for new product/process development or for firm diversification through the introduction of new products and services, they can stay motivated and continue to stay loyal to the firm. This also results in talent generation within the firm for further innovation and building competitiveness. Identifying, nurturing and rewarding entrepreneurs within a firm is a part of corporate entrepreneurship strategy to ensure that talented employees do not become restless and leave for other companies (Tribbitt, 2017).

To achieve this, it is essential to facilitate the development and management of knowledge stocks and flows between employees and organizational units as part of the corporate entrepreneurship strategy. Knowledge is information blended with experience, judgement, intuition and value that together enable the achieving of competitive advantages. Corporate entrepreneurship enables a firm to develop knowledge (which is valuable, new, unique and competitively relevant) and to use it as a continuous source of innovations to outdo its rivals (Dess, et al., 2003). A firm's intellectual capital is a key and rich source for facilitating knowledge flows required to promote corporate entrepreneurship (Hayton and Kelley, 2006). It is knowledge, skills and capabilities of individuals that together create the platform of corporate entrepreneurship within a firm (Corbett, et al., 2013).

An employer's role is to create a conducive work environment for innovation and entrepreneurial behaviour among employees. In such firms, credible innovation is likely where all employees' entrepreneurial potential is identified and nurtured, and where organizational knowledge and resources are widely shared. For top management, the challenge is to ensure the presence and continuation of an innovation-friendly internal environment (Kuratko, et al., 2014).

Empirical business researchers have identified five specific dimensions that are important determinants of a business environment conducive to innovation and entrepreneurial behavior: namely, top management support, work discretion/autonomy, rewards/reinforcement, time availability, and organizational boundaries (Hornsby, et al., 2009; Kuratko, et al., 2011). The degree of corporate entrepreneurship environment prevalent within a firm will be determined by these five broad dimensions (Kuratko, et al., 2014).

Innovation in a corporate entrepreneurial firm can be found within any of the five areas: namely, firm strategy, product offerings, served markets, internal organization, and business model (Kuratko and Audretsch, 2013). Thus, corporate entrepreneurship is more than just product development, and it can include innovations in services, channels, brands, etc. (Wolcott and Lippitz, 2007). These innovations enable a firm to differentiate itself from its industry rivals, resulting in two reference points for the firm in terms of products, markets and internal processes: how much the firm has progressed from the time prior to these innovations, and secondly, how much the firm has progressed relative to industry standards, prior to these innovations (Kuratko, et al., 2015). In the process, it will be able to assess the performance of its corporate entrepreneurship strategy involving innovations, new venture creations, and even the reorganization of business structure.

Given the above, there is no uniform strategy for corporate entrepreneurship that can be applied widely. Every firm may adopt its own innovative strategies for implementing corporate entrepreneurship. In fact, what suits one need not suit others. It would depend on management style, management goals stated in its vision and mission, the way autonomy and encouragement are given to employees, resource availability and the talent acquired and nurtured, and more.

Wolcott and Lippitz (2007) have identified two dimensions under the control of management that consistently differentiate the corporate entrepreneurship approaches adopted by companies. The first dimension is organizational ownership, and the second is resource authority. Together, the two dimensions generate a matrix containing four dominant models (Table 2.1): the opportunist (diffused ownership and ad hoc resource allocation), the enabler (diffused ownership and dedicated resources), the advocate (focussed ownership and ad hoc resource allocation), and the producer (focussed ownership and dedicated resource allocation). A firm may shift from one model to another or alternatively pursue multiple models at different levels and functions or verticals at the same time. But each of the four models calls for different kinds of leadership, processes and skill sets (Wolcott and Lippitz, 2007).

Table 2.1
Four Models of Corporate Entrepreneurship

Resource Authority	**Dedicated (Continuous)**	**The Enabler**	**The Producer**
		The company provides funding and senior executive attention to prospective projects.	The company establishes and supports a full-service group with a mandate for corporate entrepreneurship.
	Ad Hoc (Intermittent)	**The Opportunist**	**The Advocate**
		The company has no deliberate approach to corporate entrepreneurship. Internal and external networks drive concept selection and resource allocation.	The company strongly evangelizes corporate entrepreneurship, but business units provide the primary funding.
		Diffused	**Focussed**
		Organizational Ownership	

Source: Wolcott and Lippitz (2007)

For any firm, implementing corporate entrepreneurship strategy is not an easy one as it will not happen spontaneously. Actual implementation of corporate entrepreneurship strategy remains a challenge for many organizations (Kreiser, et al., 2021). It calls for conscious and consistent efforts to nurture and manage a strategic and deliberate act. Corporate entrepreneurship is not just creating a new product, or service, or a new business vertical once in a while, but transforming the way a firm grows, builds, markets and supports its offerings. Equally importantly, it would require a firm to incorporate capabilities and knowledge from outside through mergers and acquisitions, among others. Capabilities cannot be built overnight, and a corporate entrepreneurship strategy will always be a rough-and-tumble process with few guarantees. A firm cannot be guaranteed organic growth and for such firms, corporate entrepreneurship may not be the right strategy. Some attempts may succeed, and some others may fail. Corporate entrepreneurship is essentially a learning process and the success or failure may vary significantly from company to company (Wolcott and Lippitz, 2007).

Given this, it is appropriate to explore and understand what a firm ultimately achieves by pursuing corporate entrepreneurship strategy. How does it impact firm performance? What are the outcomes of the adoption of corporate entrepreneurship strategy? It is the achievement of desired outcomes which would justify the adopted strategy.

Corporate Entrepreneurship: Impact on Firm Performance and Outcomes

It is largely believed that corporate entrepreneurship has positive impacts on a firm's performance. This is because corporate entrepreneurship strategy is adopted, pursued and implemented with the key objective of gaining sustainable competitive advantage to increasingly penetrate larger markets for better firm performance. Therefore, if corporate entrepreneurship strategy is successfully pursued or implemented, it is expected to make a positive impact on firm performance.

If a firm continuously resorts to organizational restructuring, innovation and corporate venturing proactively by taking risks, it should help the firm to identify and pursue lucrative product/market opportunities, acquire superior competitive positions, and thereby steadily enhance its financial performance. Therefore, in general, it is believed that corporate entrepreneurship is positively related to firm performance and has been shown to produce multiple outcomes such as innovation, growth, learning and knowledge creation (Pennigton, 2015; Zahra, 2015). In fact, conventional wisdom states that corporate entrepreneurship results in better firm performance (Covin and Miles, 1999). It helps firms at both corporate level and business unit level (Ireland, et al., 2006).

However, empirical studies are not unanimous in their findings on the relationship between corporate entrepreneurship and firm performance (Wiklund and Shepherd, 2005; Serai, et al., 2017). The inconclusive and contradictory findings could be due to differences in firm size (large established firms vs. SMEs), differences in the nature of industries (high-tech vs. low-tech), and differences in the regions of countries considered for the study (USA or Europe or Asia). It might also be due to differences in the methods of measuring firm performance (objective performance vs. subjective performance vs. overall performance) or measuring the concept of corporate performance itself, or due to the inclusion/exclusion of mediating/control variables (Bierwerth, et al., 2015). All this boils down to the methodology applied for the selection and measurement of the variables used for the analysis, among others. To sum up, varied dimensions of corporate entrepreneurship have inclusive firm performance outcomes in different contexts.

One of the earlier studies concluded that corporate entrepreneurship was positively associated with a company's growth and profitability (Covin and Slevin, 1991), while another study argued that corporate entrepreneurship is a good predictor of growth of small firms (Covin, 1991). This brings out that firms of different sizes (large companies as well as small firms) can adopt and benefit from corporate entrepreneurship. Another empirical longitudinal study, based on data gathered from three different samples and a total of 108 firms, revealed that the relationship was not just concurrent but more importantly, the relationship was observed to grow over time, even after controlling past performance (Zahra and Covin, 1995).

This finding not just indicates the importance of adoption of corporate entrepreneurship strategy by managers; rather it emphasises the need for managers to adopt a long-term perspective in developing, managing and evaluating corporate entrepreneurship. But Zahra and Covin (1995) also noted that the external environment had a strong and persistent impact on the effectiveness of corporate entrepreneurship on firm performance. The impact is found to be better in hostile environments than in benign environments. Therefore, it is important to consider the environmental context which may enhance or stifle the impact of corporate entrepreneurship on firm performance.

Kurtako, et al. (2004), on the contrary, focussed on the internal organizational environment and stressed on the need to involve managers at all levels in designing and implementing a strategy for corporate entrepreneurship actions. It is imperative for a firm to develop an internal environment that nurtures employees' interests and commitment to creativity and innovation which would contribute to its sustainable competitive advantage. Such an internal organizational environment is an outcome of effective work by managers at all levels.

The kind of impact that corporate entrepreneurship will have on firm performance would depend on what corporate entrepreneurship would comprise and how firm performance is defined. Yang, et al. (2007), at the outset, developed a reliable and valid scale of corporate entrepreneurship and firm performance in the context of China and gathered data from 131 Chinese SMEs to identify and confirm four dimensions of corporate entrepreneurship: namely, new business venturing, innovativeness, pro-activeness and self-renewal. Subsequently, they explored the relationship of each of these components of corporate entrepreneurship with market performance. The Partial Least Square (PLS) method-based analysis revealed that three of the four dimensions of corporate entrepreneurship (i.e., excluding new business venturing) have positive and significant impacts on market performance. Among all, innovativeness turned out to be the most important driver of market performance.

Morales, et al. (2014), explored the role of technological variables and absorptive capacity (which together define the technological distinctive competencies of a firm) in influencing corporate entrepreneurship and its relationship with organizational performance. They carried out the study for 900 technology organizations within the European Union, which revealed that exploiting technologically skilled people and firms' absorptive capacity by the top management leads to the development of technologically distinctive competencies, contributing to an increase in corporate entrepreneurship. This increased corporate entrepreneurship positively contributes to firm performance.

Ambad and Wahab (2016) in the context of large-sized firms of Malaysia found that corporate entrepreneurship activities such as innovativeness, proactiveness, risk taking and corporate venturing were positively related to firm profitability and growth, in the context of environmental dynamism. The authors used survey method and secondary data from 130 large companies listed on the stock market of Bursa Malaysia and analysed the data using Partial Least Squares (PLS) method and Structural Equation Modeling (SEM). The analysis revealed that entrepreneurial orientation has a positive relationship with firm profitability but no relationship with firm growth, and corporate venturing has a positive relationship with firm growth but no relationship with firm profitability. The environmental dynamism moderated both the relationships.

Based on data from 8,280 manufacturing firms from 26 European countries, Vanacker, et al. (2017), found that corporate entrepreneurship led to enhancement of immediate, intermediate and long-term firm performance. This occurs despite weaker IP protection and weaker employee protection laws in some of these countries. Thus, perhaps for the first time, an empirical study explored the relationship between corporate entrepreneurship and firm performance with the moderating effects of IP protection and employee protection laws, with different time scales.

Bouchard and Fayolle (2018) contend that firms pursuing corporate entrepreneurship can achieve a harvest of new projects that help to generate new revenue streams. But the enhancement of economic performance is just one of the benefits that a firm is able to achieve. More importantly, according to them, there are four different kinds of benefits that would accrue to a firm practising corporate entrepreneurship: namely HR benefits (employee satisfaction and motivation), time to market (adaptability and speed), learning (individual and collective), and economic performance (revenues, innovation, and return on assets) (Figure 2.1).

Ziyae and Sadeghi (2021), in the context of Iranian financial technology companies, revealed that corporate entrepreneurship has a positive relationship with firm performance, provided those companies are entrepreneurial in nature. This implies that firms without strategic entrepreneurship are unlikely to benefit from corporate entrepreneurship strategies for improving their firm performance. That is, strategic entrepreneurship was found to have a mediating role in the relationship between corporate entrepreneurship and firm performance. It is considered a transformer for converting corporate entrepreneurship into firm performance. Therefore, entrepreneurial-minded firms should institutionalize corporate entrepreneurship in their corporate planning.

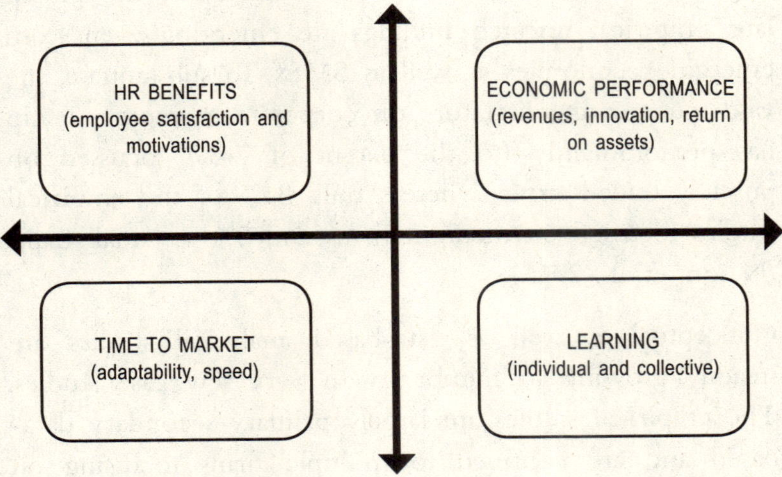

Figure 2.1: The benefits of corporate entrepreneurship

The above discussion reveals the wide diversity in the conceptualization and exploration of relationships between corporate entrepreneurship and firm performance, with or without moderating variables, in the context of both developed and developing economies. Overall, recent literature reveals that there is largely a general consensus (though not a total consensus) around the argument that successful corporate entrepreneurship leads to enhancement of firm performance (Kuratko, et al., 2004). It is against this backdrop that we derive some key research gaps, for further exploration.

Research Gaps

Empirical research on corporate entrepreneurship and firm performance is steadily growing. However, it has been predominantly confined to the developed world with a major focus on large established companies, though of late, empirical research findings are emerging even from emerging economies as well as SMEs. To substantiate, the vast and growing literature on corporate entrepreneurship has predominantly (to the extent of 74%) focussed on publicly traded firms, whereas only 21% of the empirical studies focussed on medium firms and 5% on small firms (Nason, et al., 2015).

Conceptual as well as data-based analytical studies are steadily growing in number, with very few case studies. The empirical studies are largely primary/secondary data-based and are confined to multiple firms focussing on a single country or multiple countries. The objectives, process of strategy implementation, firm performance and interrelationships between strategy and firm performance are examined in diverse ways, though there are some similarities. Though there is no unanimity, a majority of the studies have concluded that corporate entrepreneurship strategy has a positive relationship with firm performance, irrespective of how these concepts are defined, how the relationships are examined and in what contexts.

Despite all these, there still exist some research gaps that require due attention for a better understanding of these relationships. Firstly, it is yet not clear how corporate entrepreneurship strategy emerges within a firm. Does it emerge spontaneously, contributed by its innovative employees, or is it induced by the top management? Given why it emerges, does the nature of corporate entrepreneurship strategy differ between firms?

Secondly, it requires clarity to know whether the nature of corporate entrepreneurship changes as the size of a firm grows or changes over time (Nason, et al., 2015). When organizational size changes, there could be changes in the resource strength of the firm leading to a change in the strategy of corporate entrepreneurship. As a firm grows, it may change its vision and mission, and accordingly the objectives of corporate entrepreneurship strategy may change, followed by a change in the strategy itself and subsequently its impact on firm performance. However, these issues have not been explored in literature yet.

Thirdly, if corporate entrepreneurship strategy positively influences firm performance, how does it lead to a change in firm size, not just in terms of sales turnover, but more importantly also in terms of employment comprising both technical and non-technical workforce, investment and possibly exports? A steady increase in firm size, in terms of all the critical size variables, may result in a steady increase in firm-level resources leading to competitive advantages. But do such firms register higher growth as they grow over time? Empirical literature does not throw adequate light on these issues.

How does a start-up adopt corporate entrepreneurship strategy and continues to pursue it along with its growth path, over time, to emerge as the market leader and remain ahead of competition for emerging as a large public company? What are the determinants of the degree of corporate entrepreneurship prevailing in such a company? How significant is corporate entrepreneurship strategy and how does it impact firm performance for a start-up which has grown to become a unicorn and beyond? These are important research issues which have not been probed adequately in the context of either a developed economy or an emerging one. But these research issues assume added significance in the context of an emerging economy like India where ecosystems for start-ups are still evolving (Bala Subrahmanya, 2021). It is to address some of these research gaps that the present study is proposed.

Determinants, Process and Outcomes of Corporate Entrepreneurship: A Conceptual Model

Based on the understanding of core literature pertaining to corporate entrepreneurship and identifying the key variables, we propose a conceptual model of corporate entrepreneurship. Corporate entrepreneurship has emerged as an imperative strategy for a growing firm to sustain its competitive advantage and stay ahead of competition. However, adopting and sustaining corporate entrepreneurship is a challenge for a growing firm. The need to adopt and pursue corporate entrepreneurship has to be decided by the management of the firm. The management has to create a conducive environment, as well as ensure the emergence and growth of 'right talent' within the firm. It is the management vision and mission followed by an appropriate environment within the organization and the right talent that would together facilitate the adoption and sustenance of corporate entrepreneurship strategy.

The strategy implementation process would involve periodic: (i) organizational restructuring, (ii) innovation and (iii) corporate venturing. Towards this end, the management should constantly encourage new ideas of employees, expose them to multiple functions through periodic business restructuring, devote resources for ideation and innovations, provide freedom of action for risk-taking with no punitive actions for failures, and encourage corporate venturing through the creation of new business verticals for diversification on a constant basis. The management should be willing to accept failures and encourage success, to achieve sustained competitive advantage and enhanced firm performance on a continuous basis. In the process, the firm may acquire outside start-ups, for entering new business verticals and for possessing the required talent. At the same time, the firm might generate new start-ups through the exit of some of its employees who have gained confidence, resources, talent, networks, and market knowledge, with or without any support from the firm.

The outcomes of pursuing corporate entrepreneurship strategy may be success or failure. The success of corporate entrepreneurship strategy may emerge in different forms such as innovative products/services, increased employment, increased investment, new business verticals, and increased sales turnover. The failure of the strategy would reflect in lack of innovation, lack of new business verticals, moderate or negligible growth in employment, investment and sales turnover. The relationship between the critical variables relating to corporate entrepreneurship strategy is presented in the form of a conceptual model in Figure 2.2.

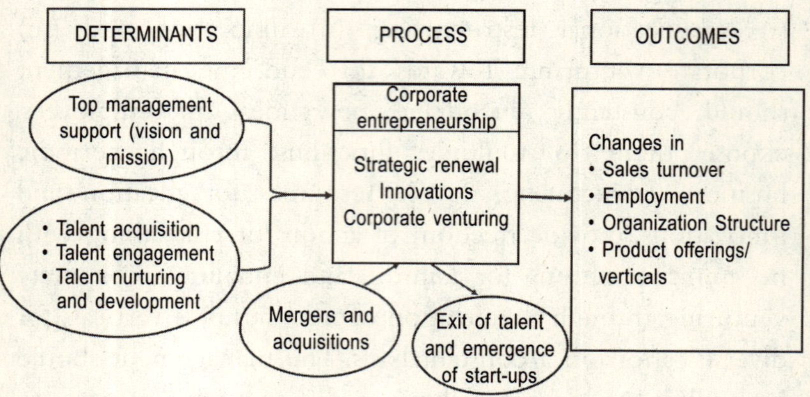

Figure 2.2: Corporate entrepreneurship: Determinants, process and outcomes

It is against this conceptual framework that we carried out an investigation of our research objectives with reference to the scope of the study, by means of the methods of analysis, stated in the previous chapter.

3

FLIPKART: FROM START-UP ENTREPRENEURSHIP TO CORPORATE ENTREPRENEURSHIP

Introduction

Flipkart's growth process began with its formation in October 2007 (*Business Connect*, 2021: Rajan, 2020; Dalal, 2019a). Though Flipkart started as an online bookstore, it steadily and continuously diversified its business verticals as it grew alongside the business of online book sales. In the process, it has introduced innovative business strategies, diversified its product portfolios, experimented by entering new product lines, though it discontinued or withdrew from some of them due to inadequate success, acquired multiple tech start-ups in diverse business verticals, while experiencing the exit of many talented executives who subsequently created their own start-ups. In the whole process, Flipkart steadily increased its visibility and credibility by continuously increasing its customer (buyers) base on the one hand, and merchant (sellers) base on the other, in the Indian e-commerce industry and beyond.

A Brief History: Chronology of Events

Broadly, the growth process of Flipkart can be divided into two parts: its founding in 2007 (Dalal, 2019b) and subsequent growth till 2018, and its growth since the investment by Walmart as a major shareholder of Flipkart in 2018 (Business Connect, 2021) till now. The chronology of events initiated by the founders and management broadly falls under the four functional areas of management: namely, production and operations including supply chain and logistics, human resources (talent acquisition), finance (raising funds regularly), and marketing (steady market penetration). Together, these events influenced and impacted supply as well as demand for the long-term growth of Flipkart.

Phase I (2007–2018): Emergence and Growth

Flipkart was one of the earliest Indian unicorns, achieving the unicorn valuation of US$1 billion in 2012 (Banerjee, Sayed, Startup Talky, 2022). It was founded by two young graduates of IIT Delhi, Sachin Bansal and Binny Bansal. Both had worked in two different tech start-ups, followed by stints at Amazon Web services, before setting up their own start-up, Flipkart in Bangalore, the start-up capital of India. (Though both founders hailed from Chandigarh, India, and share the same surname, they are not related.) At first, they planned to launch a 'comparison search engine' offering product reviews that would enable customers to look at various alternatives available online, and choose their online purchase (*Business Connect*, 2021; Dalal, 2019b).

But soon they realized that there was a huge gap in the e-commerce sector in India, and there existed opportunities for marketing and selling books online. Both were confident of the tremendous potential of e-commerce in India, though they were unsure and therefore did not aim at any specific number. But they had a couple of critical challenges in setting up their new venture. Firstly, they simply did not know how to go-to-market in the form of search engine optimization (SEO), which is a fundamental part of digital marketing. In simple terms, it means the process of improving a start-up's site to increase its visibility when people search online for products or services related to its business. The better visibility a start-up's pages have in search results, the more likely it will garner attention and attract prospective and existing customers to its business and acquire sales. The Bansals learned this from a couple of start-up founders.

Secondly, they had not raised any money. Therefore, the start-up was created with ploughing in their own seed capital of INR 400,000/USD$ 4,790 (Business Inspection, 2021; Chakraborty, 2017). Thirdly, hiring key employees was a challenge. Ambur Iyyappa was hired as a delivery manager, becoming Flipkart's first employee (*WION* web, 2018). Thus, they overcame the initial key challenges of technology for digital marketing, finance and human resources. Flipkart started its operations from a two-bedroom apartment in Koramangala, Bangalore, in October 2007.

Sachin Bansal, CEO and co-founder of Flipkart, assumed the role of Executive Chairman and Binny Bansal, COO and co-founder of Flipkart, assumed the role of Chief Executive Officer (Menon, *Man's World*, 2016), marking the beginning of the entrepreneurial journey of the two founders. They adopted a 'customer first' strategy in all their firm-building strategies since then. Within a year, they acquired a customer base that enabled them to gain some financial stability. Slowly and steadily, Flipkart gained visibility and prominence. By 2008, it was receiving about 100 orders daily.

Flipkart was initially funded (INR 1 million/US$12,000 in 2009) by Ashish Gupta, founder of Junglee and Helion Venture Partners funds (*Mint*, 2018; Chakraborty, 2017). In 2009, for the first time, Flipkart obtained a round of external finance of US$1 million from Accel Partners, a venture capital firm (Chakraborty, 2017; Flipkart Stories-Timeline). At that time, Flipkart had 150 employees (Flipkart Stories-Timeline) and three offices across India – in Bangalore, Mumbai and New Delhi. By the end of 2009, Flipkart could sell books worth INR 40 million/US$479,000 (Business Inspection, 2021; Varun 2020a, Varun 2020b).

Flipkart reached its first major milestone when Tiger Global invested Series B funding to the tune of US$10 million in 2010 (Crunchbase-Series B; Chakraborty, 2017). In the same year, Flipkart acquired a Bangalore-based social book discovery service, WeRead (Flipkart Stories-Timeline, Business Inspection, 2021), prompted by the business synergies between the two firms. Perhaps it was the first acquisition of an Indian tech start-up by another Indian tech start-up in India's start-up history.

This acquisition enabled Flipkart to gain further strength and visibility in the Indian market. It was at this juncture that Flipkart decided to diversify into the selling of electronics products online but did not find it viable, and therefore withdrew from this business line. Customers were willing to pay online for books since the amount involved was much smaller compared to electronic products, which were ten times costlier than their most expensive book. This made Flipkart work on an alternative strategy to win over customer trust, which necessitated brand building and establishing brand trust.

It was in 2010 that Flipkart introduced cash on delivery (CoD) (Flipkart Stories) and a 30-day 'no questions asked' replacement policy—the first of its kind in India, truly a business innovation (Keshavdev, 2021). However, Flipkart faced challenges in implementing it due to inadequate, delayed and unsatisfactory logistics then prevalent in the country. The Net Promoter Score (NPS) for CoD was not up to Flipkart's expectations. NPS is considered a key indicator of loyalty, which can range from -100 to +100, and it measures customers' willingness to recommend a company's products/services to others.

Flipkart Logistics, which became Ekart subsequently, was thus born. This enabled the firm to win over the trust of consumers—particularly those who were wary of making payments in advance for things to be delivered later—significantly contributing to the growth of business as well as revenue. The introduction of CoD emerged as a game changer. One of the reasons Flipkart took off was that they brought in cash on delivery (Nilekani, 2016). Perhaps this laid the foundation for Flipkart's subsequent steady growth.

At the beginning of 2011, Flipkart's revenue stood at INR 750 million/US$8.9 million (*Business Inspection*, 2021). In June 2011, Flipkart raised Series C funding of US$20 million from its existing investor, Tiger Global (Chakraborty, 2017; Crunchbase, Series C; VC Circle 2011[a]).

In late 2011 Flipkart launched its 'kids as adults' advertisement, a major marketing innovation. The campaign was a huge hit—the children effectively managed to sell the idea to end users. Dubbed as 'No Kidding No Worries', the Flipkart Kids campaign featured ads that were considered funny and memorable. They were initiated first on social media—introduced to Facebook and Twitter audiences. Based on the feedback received, these ads were later refined and introduced to Indian television audiences (Venugopal, 2017). This made a huge impact on consumers, enabling Flipkart to surpass targets in customers, traffic volume and sales. The Flipkart Kids campaign that ran from 2011 to 2013 elevated the brand into the national imagination. In 2016, after a break during which the brand adopted other creative approaches, the kids made a comeback.

In 2011, Flipkart made its second acquisition, Mime360, a digital distribution platform (Flipkart Stories, Vikas, 2011). Following this, Flipkart made another acquisition, Bollywood site Chakpak's content catalogue (Reuters, 2011). This acquisition enabled Flipkart to offer digital content to its customers in the form of editorial and user-generated content for a vast number of Indian movies, through the already acquired Mime360. Thus, the acquisition of the Mime360 digital platform followed by Chakpak's digital catalogue was a well-thought-out complementary strategy to gain further ground in the e-commerce space in the country.

Following this acquisition, Flipkart launched its DRM-free online music* store Flyte in 2012 (Flipkart Stories-Timeline; The Next Web, 2018). Flyte was later shut down in June 2013 (Firstpost, 2013). However, this failure did not deter Flipkart management from achieving further business diversification through acquisitions. In 2012, Flipkart acquired Letsbuy, an online electronics retailer (Flipkart Stories-Timeline, Sharma-*Times of India*, 2012). Thereby, Flipkart acquired a firm footing in the online sale of electronics products.

In 2012, Flipkart became a unicorn with its valuation exceeding US$1 billion (Chakraborty, 2017). In early 2012, Flipkart received funding of US$150 million from South African tech major Naspers. In addition, Flipkart raised US$200 million in mid-2013 and another US$160 million from Morgan Stanley, Sofina, Vulcan Capital and Dragoneer (Chakraborty, 2017).

In July 2013, Flipkart diversified into digital payments platform by launching its payment gateway, PayZippy, under a separate firm, Flipkart Payment Gateway Services (FPGS) Private Limited, and started with payment solutions to merchants (Mehta, 2013). However, the payment gateway was later closed down. Instead, Flipkart invested in JiGrahak's ngpay, a mobile app that enabled customers

---

*DRM-free music refers to music that is not protected by Digital Rights Management (DRM) technology. DRM-free music means you can play it on any device. There are no restrictions on which devices or platforms you can use to listen to the music.

to buy flight tickets, book movie tickets, purchase goods and services, and make payments through mobile phones (Sareen, *Inc42*, 2014). The partnership was expected to gain from the technical talent of ngpay to drive innovation in digital payments, with features and products that provided a competitive end-to-end customer experience, to redefine the digital payments ecosystem in India. Soon thereafter, Flipkart also acquired payment services start-up FX Mart. Started in 2013, FX Mart offered electronic payments, foreign exchange and travel services, and held a prepaid wallet license issued by the RBI (Flipkart Stories-Timeline; *Inc42* (2015). This allowed Flipkart to offer a digital wallet on its app, eliminating the reliance on external wallet providers and avoiding associated fees. These investments in ngpay and FX Mart together enabled Flipkart to gain a foothold in the digital payments space—an initial step towards the adoption of Industry 4.0.

In February 2014, Flipkart worked with Motorola Mobility as it explored India's growing online commerce market for the sale of Moto G smartphone. This partnership helped Flipkart gain an upper hand in the sale of mobile phones over the next couple of years. Motorola continued its collaboration with Flipkart for the sale of Moto E, a phone targeted primarily towards emerging markets like India (Divekar, 2014). This was followed by Indian launches of other smartphones such as Xiaomi Mi 3 in July 2014, Redmi 1S and Redmi Note in the later part of 2014, and Micromax's Yu Yunique in 2017. Flipkart was able to offer a new category to consumers as they started looking at buying mobile phones online. Later, Motorola extended the product categories and introduced Motorola e6s, smart TVs and home appliances as well (Motorola-Flipkart, 2022; DT Next, 2020).

Flipkart continued on start-up acquisition to propel its growth. With the acquisition of Myntra, an online fashion retailer in 2014, Flipkart gained a major boost in the online sale of fashion garments (*Times of India*, 2014 [a]). Myntra has continued to be a separate brand of Flipkart, focussing on separate market segments since then. The sourcing of garment merchandise was strengthened when Flipkart invested a minority stake in Arvind Fashion Limited's newly formed subsidiary, Arvind Youth Brands, which owned Flying Machine brand, at a later date (Flipkart Stories-Press Release; Arvind Fashions Press Release).

Following the acquisition of Myntra in 2014, Flipkart raised US$210 million in Series F from DST Global. The valuation then stood at US$2.6 billion. Soon thereafter, Flipkart witnessed a whopping US$1 billion funding in Series G round from GIC Singapore and existing backers like Naspers, DST Global and Tiger Global. As a result, the valuation shot up to reach US$7 billion within three months. Before the end of the year, Flipkart raised another US$700 million in Series H from hedge funds like Greenoaks, Steadview Capital, sovereign wealth fund Qatar Investment Authority, and mutual fund T Rowe Price. Flipkart's valuation further increased to more than US$11 billion (Crunchbase Series H; Crunchbase Series F; Crunchbase Series G; Chakraborty, 2017). Thus, Flipkart graduated to become a 'decacorn' (a company valued at more than US$10 billion) from a unicorn in just about two years.

In 2014, as a major online sales acceleration exercise, Flipkart introduced the 'Big Billion Days Sale' on October 6 to commemorate the company's anniversary and the Deepavali festival (Dalal, 2019b). This exercise turned out to be hugely successful, as it generated a surge of traffic leading to a sale of US$100 million in just 10 hours. The success of, and the response to, the event pushed Flipkart to continue the Big Billion Days Sale as a multi-day event subsequently, with better tech preparedness to manage customer traffic. It has become an annual multi-day event since then. This was another major business innovation introduced by Flipkart, unprecedented in the Indian context; subsequently it was imitated by competitors in different forms in the Indian e-commerce market, which speaks volumes about Flipkart's 'market innovativeness'.

In October 2014, Flipkart entered into a strategic partnership by acquiring Jeeves Consumer Services Pvt. Ltd, which provides hassle-free after-sales services on large home appliances and electronics including DVD players, TVs, washing machines, food processors or laptops (Dalal, 2014). This was expected to help Flipkart in two important ways: in launching home appliance products under its own label (for which after-sales service could be effectively provided), and if offline retailers stopped offering guarantees, Flipkart would be able to offer them with the help of Jeeves. With Jeeves, Flipkart could serve customers products from a category like large appliances and build trustworthiness, with regard to installation, demonstrations, service touch points and warranties. Thus, Flipkart further shaped and enabled customer behaviour towards a new category, by entering into the space of after-sales service and installation business. This is obviously in line with their customer-first strategy, which also aimed at increasing market penetration and sales.

In 2015, Flipkart bought a stake in auctions start-up WeHive Technologies (Your Story, 2015), followed by a co-investment in online freight booking service Zinka (ITVoice, 2022; Singh-*Inc42*, 2015). The latter was a move to further improve its logistics and supply chain capabilities. This was followed by its investment, along with its largest investor Tiger Global, in online home rentals start-up NestAway (Shrivastava and Chanchani, 2015). In March 2015, Flipkart acquired Bangalore-based global mobile network AdIquity, which owned and operated mobile advertising platform AdIquity (Peer, 2015). AdIquity, which initially started with the now-defunct local search engine Guruji.com back in 2006, enabled mobile app developers and publishers to earn revenues by leveraging their mobile inventory. It also helped ad agencies, ad networks and other media buyers acquire global mobile traffic. The acquisition was expected to empower Flipkart's external marketing.

In April 2015 Flipkart acquired Appiterate (Flipkart Stories; YourStory), a Delhi-based mobile marketing automation start-up. This acquisition occurred after Flipkart developed a commercial partnership with the latter. The initial rounds of interactions with Appiterate enabled Flipkart management to realize that more value can be achieved by integrating Appiterate within Flipkart instead of having an external relationship. Appiterate was primarily engaged in sending personalized (push) notifications based on predictive analytics to potential customers (on behalf of its customers, who were leading e-commerce companies), through its platform.

This helped Flipkart reach out to potential customers in a personalized way through a tech-enabled service. Another move towards the adoption of Industry 4.0.

The Flipkart strategy of acquiring early-stage start-ups was confined to India till 2015. It extended its acquisition strategy abroad, when it acquired the Silicon Valley-based artificial intelligence start-up F7 Labs in June 2015 (TechStory-BIDKAR, 2017; Ahmed, 2017; Ghoshal, 2018). This marked the beginning of the 'internationalization phase' of Flipkart's growth process. The objective of acquiring F7 Labs was to employ the latest technologies for its datasets and gain insights into customers' shopping behaviour. Ever since its acquisition, F7 Labs has been helping Flipkart improve its business processes and enhance the shopping experience for its customers through data-led insights, from the nature of their 'search queries to how they evaluate products before clicking the buy button'. These insights have helped their product teams optimize the experience for customers and sellers—one more step towards adopting Industry 4.0.

In early 2015, Flipkart advised customers to use its mobile app for online purchases, and blocked access to its website on mobile devices, but it did not receive an encouraging response. Instead, Flipkart launched a new mobile-based website, Flipkart lite, in November 2015, which runs on smartphone web browsers (Eshwar, 2015). The new mobile site was made accessible only via Google Chrome on Android phones. This was prompted due to an increasingly large proportion of Flipkart sales coming through the mobile app by then.

In December 2015, Flipkart acquired a stake in digital

mapping firm MapmyIndia (a leading firm which has digital map data, GPS investigation, tracking, location-based apps and GIS solutions) (MapmyIndia Press Release, 2015). The objective of this acquisition was to strengthen Flipkart's overall supply chain logistics. The deployment of location intelligence capabilities of MapmyIndia across Flipkart's logistics network would strengthen its first-mile pickup and last-mile delivery operations. It would also enable Flipkart to leverage MapmyIndia's data for better address verification, real-time shipment tracking, facility mapping and theft minimization. Location is becoming increasingly important to understand consumer behaviour, and MapmyIndia's database across metros, cities and towns was considered an asset for Flipkart for hyperlocal distribution and warehouses. This was another right move towards Industry 4.0 adoption for obtaining sustainable competitive advantage (Chanchani and Dave, 2015).

The acquisition trend continued in 2016 with the acquisition of online retailer Jabong.com (Flipkart Stories; Binny's post) from Rocket Internet through Flipkart's unit, Myntra.com (Verma, 2016). Jabong was a major competitor to Myntra in the online sale of fashion garments, particularly till 2014. Therefore, this acquisition would have further consolidated the position of Flipkart to emerge as the leading online seller of fashion garments in the fast-growing Indian e-market.

In 2016, Flipkart also witnessed a transition in its management as Sachin Bansal was succeeded by Binny Bansal as CEO (Flipkart Stories), who later became the Group CEO in 2017. He was the Chief Operating Officer (COO) of Flipkart till then. However, the growth strategy and journey of Flipkart continued unabated, with steady expansion through acquisitions.

Flipkart's position in the digital payments space got a fillip when it acquired PhonePe in April 2016 (Chathurvedula, 2016). PhonePe was a start-up initiated by former Flipkart executives in December 2015. The acquisition of PhonePe was in line with Flipkart's focus on driving innovation on the payments front and it added to Flipkart's position in the digital payments space, gained with the acquisitions of ngpay and FX Mart. Facilitating digital payments was considered a step to overcome the hurdles for mass adoption of online shopping in India. Therefore, the acquisitions of ngpay, FX Mart and PhonePe would have given a boost to Flipkart sales, since 2016.

In May 2016, Flipkart's logistics arm Ekart launched courier services to deliver parcels to its customers and streamline the fragmented courier market across the country (BGR. in, 2016). The service would allow users to drop a pin for pick-up and delivery addresses on Ekart's mapping platform, which would have RFID (radio frequency identification) and global positioning system (GPS) for real-time tracking of the courier's journey. The service also offered consumers benefits of 24×7 online booking on mobile and website, slotted doorstep pick-up, free packaging, pricing and delivery time. The objective was to provide value, reliability, convenience and speed to its customers—a direct outcome of the adoption of many dimensions of Industry 4.0 by Flipkart then.

In May 2016, Flipkart also introduced another innovative financing solution to its customers, that is, 'no cost EMI':

a monthly instalment-based payment scheme with no processing fee, no hidden costs, no down payment and no interest payout. Flipkart's no-cost EMI was a first step towards making online shopping truly affordable for the masses (Nair, 2016). In September 2017, this was extended to 'EMI on debit cards' scheme (Flipkart Stories, 2017). This assumes significance in the Indian context because credit card ownership remains low and getting small personal loans from the banking system is a hassle. This was a major step in transforming desire into demand for lower-income customers.

In January 2017, Kalyan Krishnamurthy was appointed CEO of Flipkart, taking over from Binny Bansal. Kalyan, a former Tiger Global executive, had an earlier stint in Flipkart as an interim Chief Financial Officer from May 2013 to November 2014 (Gupta, 2017). He rejoined Flipkart in June 2016. He later facilitated the Walmart-Flipkart deal wherein Walmart acquired 77% stake in the latter, in August 2018.

The Flipkart strategy of start-up acquisitions continued with Kalyan at the helm. In January 2017, Flipkart invested US$2 million in TinyStep, a parenting information start-up. TinyStep operates a parenting service that focusses on providing information, advice and a social network for parents. The network covers pregnancy and baby and toddler stages to help guide would-be parents through the stressful period that comes with welcoming a newborn into the world. It also provides a 'mums only' segment where women can ask questions with a higher level of privacy (Russell, 2017).

In May 2017, to further boost its mobile phone sales, Flipkart introduced a 'buyback guarantee' offer on the purchase of smartphones. Under this offer, Flipkart promised to buy back a smartphone at an assured price, ensuring maximum return to its customers (Banerjee, 2017). This implied an assurance and a guaranteed value for customers' existing smartphones, if and when they buy their next smartphone on the site, irrespective of technology disruptions and market fluctuations. A year after (May 2018), Flipkart introduced a 'complete mobile protection plan' which included a range of benefits that went beyond standard brand warranties, including repairs throughout the lifecycle of the product, and pick-up-and-drop services from customers' doorstep (Flipkart Stories, 2018). This was a major initiative to win over complete customer trust.

In June 2017, Flipkart introduced yet another revolutionary market promotion strategy by launching the 'buy now, pay later' scheme so customers could buy products on the platform on credit (Pitchiah, 2017). The offer is applicable only to 'Flipkart Assured' products, and available on products of select sellers. For payment, Flipkart sends SMSes and app notifications to users on the 1st of every month, along with the bill details and payment link (Flipkart Pay Later TnC). This is, again, another strategy to convert consumer desire into consumer demand by bridging the gap between access to credit and consumers' aspirations. The scheme was planned to get extended to all of its customers in the future.

In September 2017, Flipkart acquired F1 Info Solutions, one of the largest third-party service providers in the Indian electronics market. F1 Info Solutions had 158 owned and franchised centres and nearly 1,000 employees at the time of its acquisition. F1 was engaged in the repair and servicing of mobile phones, which suited Flipkart's growth ambition to enter the refurbished goods market (Arakali, 2018). This led to the building of a reverse supply chain by Flipkart—a series of activities required to retrieve a used product from customers and either reuse it or dispose of it. Flipkart being the leading platform for smartphone retail in India, understood the pattern of customer purchases characterized by the periodic replacement of old smartphones with new ones with new additional features, after a few years. To cash in on this, Flipkart introduced a 'smartphone exchange program' which led to flooding of the return supply chain with old smartphones in good working condition.

With Jeeves and F1 Info Solutions providing a strong network of technicians and engineers on the ground, Flipkart started paying more attention to issues of 'product returns' through technician visits and product validations. This enabled Flipkart to minimize the losses incurred due to product returns by filling the crucial gap between online and offline markets. Flipkart obtained what other online sellers do not have and what offline sellers have, i.e., the personal touch of service technicians. Thus, products sold by Flipkart are installed by Jeeves and F1 technicians by visiting the customers: minor technical or usage issues are resolved on the spot. In addition, Jeeves F1 built a network of walk-in service centres so that customers who needed more help with their products could visit these (Sreekumar, 2019).

Flipkart created an internal unit called AIforIndia, a major attempt to put machine learning (ML) and artificial intelligence (AI) at the core of its business, after its acquisition of Silicon Valley-based firm, F7 Labs (in 2015)

(*Moneycontrol*, 2018; Mendonca, 2017; Ghoshal, 2018). The objective was to build internal capabilities within India in ML and AI, and to bridge technology gaps relative to its competitors. This move was aimed at further consolidation and adoption of Industry 4.0.

The chronology of key events from October 2007 till April 2018 is briefly presented in Table 3.1. It broadly covers Flipkart's origin, in terms of co-founders and management, periodic fundraising, creation of new ventures and business vertical diversification, M&As, partnerships, process/market/financial innovations, management change, and co-investments.

Table 3.1
Chronology of Events
(from October 2007 to April 2018)

Calendar	Event
October 2007	Creation of the start-up as Flipkart with Sachin Bansal as CEO and Binny Bansal as COO (with own funds of INR 400,000)
2009	First external funding of INR 1 million obtained
	Obtained funding of US$1 million
2010	Obtained Series B funding of US$10 million
	First M&A of WeRead
	Diversifies into sale of electronic goods but withdraws
	'Cash on delivery' and '30-day no questions asked replacement' introduced
	Flipkart Logistics created (which later became Ekart Logistics)

2011	Raises Series C funding of US$20 million
	'Kids as adults' ad launched
	M&As of Mime360 and Chakpak's digital catalogue
2012	Online music store Flyte launched but shut down later
	M&A of Letsbuy and re-enters into the sale of electronics goods
	Flipkart attains unicorn status
2013	Raises funding of US$200 million
	Raises funding of US$160 million
	Diversifies into digital payments by launching payment gateway PayZippy, as a new venture, but shuts down later
2014	Develops collaboration with Motorola for exclusive marketing of Motorola smartphones
	Sale of Xiaomi Mi3, Redmi 1S, and Redmi Note
	Acquires Myntra, which continues to maintain its separate identity since then
	Invests in Arvind Youth Brands
	Raises Series F funding of US$210 million
	Raises Series G funding of US$1 billion
	Raises Series F funding of US$700 million
	Introduces 'Big Billion Days Sale'
	Strategic partnership with Jeeves Consumer Services Ltd. Enters 'after-sales service' business

2015	Buys a stake in WeHive Technologies
	Co-invests in Zinka, a logistics start-up
	Invests in NestAway, an online home rental start-up
	M&A of AdIquity, a mobile advertising platform
	M&A of Appiterate, a mobile marketing automation start-up
	Acquires F-7 Labs, a Silicon Valley-based AI start-up
	Acquires a stake in MapmyIndia, a digital mapping firm
2016	M&A of Jabong.com through Myntra
	Binny Bansal takes over as CEO from Sachin Bansal
	Acquires PhonePe, a digital payment start-up created by ex-Flipsters
	Launches courier services through Ekart Logistics
	Launches 'No cost EMI' and 'EMI on debit card' schemes
2017	Kalyan Krishnamurthy appointed CEO
	Invests in TinyStep, a parenting information start-up
	Introduces 'buyback guarantee' offer on purchase of smartphones
	Introduces 'buy now, pay later' scheme
	Acquires F1 Info Solutions
2018	Introduces 'complete mobile protection plan'
	Creates a new venture within, called AIforIndia

Phase II (2018 onwards): Investment by Walmart and Subsequent Growth

In May 2018, Walmart signed definitive agreements to become the largest shareholder in Flipkart Group. The investment was expected to help accelerate Flipkart's customer-focussed mission to transform commerce in India through technology. The necessary official approvals for acquiring 77% stake in Flipkart by Walmart were obtained in August 2018 (Dalal, 2019; ET Bureau, 2018). This marked the beginning of the second phase of Flipkart's growth. Binny Bansal, one of the two co-founders, continued as a minor shareholder and a board member, whereas Sachin Bansal, the other co-founder, exited completely (Dalal, 2019).

In August 2018, Flipkart launched its new portal, 2GUD.com, to sell certified refurbished goods (including mobile phones, laptops and tablets, among others) at 'low-cost prices' with a 3 to 12 months' warranty. This was considered to be Flipkart's first-ever independent platform for refurbished goods in India (Flipkart Press Release (2018): Flipkart launches 2GUD; Agarwal, *Mint*, 2018). First of all, this enabled customers to sell their used products at the 'best possible value'. Secondly, this platform played a significant role in transforming 'a new market of used products' into 'demand'. Thus, it has resolved the affordability problem of a lot of 'low-income group' customers. The service of 2GUD.com involved doorstep delivery of platform-based purchases. The platform also allowed customers to return their products. Thus, the major contribution of 2GUD.com has been in the form of overcoming the 'trust deficit' and 'inconvenience' that existed in the refurbished goods market.

In fact, 2GUD.com has been ably backed by the technical expertise of Jeeves F1, especially the latter's capabilities in the electronics segment. The combination of 2GUD.com and Jeeves F1 has facilitated standardization in the refurbished market in India, which was till then operating predominantly in the unorganized sector. The opening of 'refurbishment centres' by Jeeves F1 has not only created employment for many local low-skilled technicians but also enabled them to upgrade their skills by working at a state-of-the-art facility. This could be considered a major contribution of Flipkart in (i) upskilling the unorganized sector labour force and (ii) transforming unorganized-sector employment into organized-sector employment in India.

A significant outcome of the whole process is Flipkart's ability to provide end-to-end coverage of the supply chain, which would make the entry of any new foreign brands into the competitive Indian market fairly smooth. This is because Flipkart can handle the 'entire lifecycle of a product'.

In August 2018, Flipkart acquired Liv.ai, a speech recognition AI start-up which has built a platform that converts speech to text in 10 Indian languages (Flipkart Stories, Announcements, 2018). After acquisition. Liv.ai became Flipkart's centre of excellence for voice solutions, to help the end-to-end conversational shopping experience for its customers. The objective was to lure more and more vernacular language customers to the Flipkart platform for online purchases, another major marketing move with the use of deep technologies. This acquisition further strengthened Flipkart's adoption of Industry 4.0.

To give further boost to its AI and ML capabilities, in

September 2018, Flipkart acquired Israel-based retail analytics company Upstream Commerce, primarily for its technology that would allow Flipkart to offer real-time pricing and product analytics (Team Flipkart Stories (2021); Hector, 2018). Based in Tel Aviv, Upstream Commerce builds cloud-based, automated competitive pricing and product analysis technology that would help sellers optimize their product assortment and pricing strategies and find gaps in the market to serve customers better. Upstream's 20 employees became a part of the Flipkart workforce but continued to work out of Israel. With this, Israel, a country with a vibrant and innovative start-up ecosystem, became a part of Flipkart's global centres for future data science work. The acquisitions of both Liv.ai and Upstream Commerce were in line with Flipkart's vision to promote e-commerce through technology innovations, through in-house efforts as well as the inorganic route.

In July 2019, Flipkart along with Axis Bank launched a co-branded credit card powered by Mastercard (with 5% cashback on purchases) (Isi, 2019). This was done to reap the high-potential credit card market, which had been growing at a fast pace, though with a small base. The objective was to provide access to formal credit to a wider population of the country. The credit card was introduced with some unique features which included, among others, credit of cashback directly in the monthly billing statement. This would have given another boost to sales through new customers.

Till early 2019, Flipkart used to invest directly in other start-ups in the digital field. However, in 2019, Flipkart set up an early-stage investment arm of Flipkart, with a

$100 million fund to back early-stage start-ups in India and thereby support the ecosystem to build innovative solutions for the next wave of internet users (Flipkart Ventures). Thus, Flipkart created an exclusive venture fund for making speedy investment decisions and investments. This has a two-fold objective: (i) to promote the digital start-up ecosystem, since obtaining funds has been a serious challenge for early-stage ventures, particularly the innovative ones which show potential to solve real-world issues through disruptive technologies, and (ii) to explore developing partnerships or even acquisitions, if their technology, product and/or talent are considered complementary to the core interests of the parent firm. Flipkart Ventures' focus would be on e-commerce, fintech and other complementary fields in the digital sector.

In July 2019, Flipkart Samarth was launched to bring Indian artisans, weavers, handicraft producers, women entrepreneurs, and differently abled entrepreneurs onto e-commerce (Flipkart Stories, 2019). This is an important step towards providing national market access to unorganized and underserved communities of India. Flipkart Samarth has been designed to support artisans in their e-commerce journey, from onboarding until they gain familiarity with the online selling process themselves. The initiative has also taken steps to deal with their common obstacles such as lack of access to working capital, poor infrastructure, and inadequate training. In this regard, Flipkart has decided to work closely with NGOs, government bodies and livelihood missions to reach a large number of rural entrepreneurs in the country. This is a much-needed initiative to promote the under-supported artisan and small-scale sellers of India.

In August 2019, Flipkart partnered with Authentic Brands to license and distribute global lifestyle brand Nautica in India (Shrivastava, 2019). The Nautica partnership would allow local production in India, enabling a lot of ecosystem players like sellers and manufacturers to make exclusive lines for India along with launching the brand's global range in the country. The overall objective is to reach out to a larger customer market for both in the sector.

In November 2019, Flipkart invested $4 million and acquired a stake in EasyRewardz, a loyalty points management start-up (EasyRewardz; *Times of India*-PTI, 2019). EasyRewardz is a business-to-business loyalty management platform that helps brands and banks manage loyalty points. The entire backend of customers wanting to earn, burn and redeem loyalty points is taken care of by EasyRewardz. Flipkart was looking to leverage the EasyRewardz loyalty platform to build loyalty solutions through which points could be used across online and offline merchants.

In December 2019, Flipkart bought a minority stake in B2B logistics start-up Shadowfax (Flipkart Corporate, Singh-TechCrunch, 2015). Shadowfax operates an unusually built business-to-business logistics network in more than 300 cities in India. The start-up works with neighbourhood stores to use their real estate to store inventory, and a large network of freelancers for the delivery. Anyone with a bicycle or a bike or a truck can join the Shadowfax platform and deliver items. This capability enabled Flipkart to do on-demand categories delivering smartphones, fashion, grocery, etc., in less than 120 minutes. It also opened up the potential to build newer categories like dairy, meat, fruits, vegetables, and pharmacy using Shadowfax's technology, as well as kirana network. In the same month, Flipkart also invested in Ninjacart, a fresh-produce supply chain firm. Flipkart later used both Ninjacart and Shadowfax to build last-mile support for its hyperlocal service 'Quick', launched after six months (Team Flipkart Stories, 2021; Ninjacart Media; ET Tech, 2021; Yourstory, Talgeri, 2022).

In August 2020, Flipkart went a step further in the promotion of digital start-ups. It launched a start-up accelerator programme known as Flipkart Leap (Flipkart Press Release, 2021). The objective was to identify B2C and B2B start-ups and help them scale through an intensive 16-week programme with an equity grant of US$25,000 (*Mint*, 2020a). The programme identified five themes to shortlist relevant start-ups. The themes included design and make for India, innovation in digital commerce, technologies to empower the retail ecosystem, supply chain management and logistics, and enabling relevant deep tech applications. The themes have been identified to tap into solutions in the technology and consumer internet space. The Flipkart Leap programme graduated its first cohort in July 2021 with eight start-ups, which enabled those start-ups to raise further funding (Flipkart Stories-Leap Cohort; Flipkart Leap Press Release, 2020; Flipkart Press Release, 2021; Flipkart Press Release, 2021b).

In July 2020, building on its technology capabilities and supply chain infrastructure, Flipkart launched its hyperlocal service Flipkart Quick, which promised to deliver a handpicked assortment of more than 2,000 products in categories varying from groceries and dairy and meat products, to mobiles, electronics accessories, stationery items and home accessories from local Flipkart hubs in just 90 minutes (*Mint*, 2020b). Flipkart Quick would adopt a latitude and longitude approach that would not only narrow down the location to be more precise but also result in sharper delivery time. Instead of the traditional model of using a pin-code system to identify the delivery location, which could span a larger area, Flipkart Quick would use innovative and advanced technology for location mapping.

In August 2020, Flipkart launched a digital B2B platform called Flipkart Wholesale to connect local manufacturers with retailers and bring the entire wholesale marketplace at their fingertips using technology (Shrivastava, 2020). The newly created digital B2B platform aimed at meeting the needs of kiranas and MSMEs by providing these small businesses a wide range of selections at a significant value, powered by technology to make their lives easier. As a result, these small businesses now had one-stop access to an extensive selection of products (in grocery, general merchandise, fashion garments), supplemented with driven recommendations for stock selection, delivered through a fast and reliable network to drive greater efficiencies. In addition, small businesses were offered an easy credit facility to manage cash flow, a wide range of Flipkart-assured quality products, simple and convenient order returns, and speedy product delivery directly to their shops with an easy order-tracking facility. This was expected to give a boost to the MSME ecosystem in India.

In November 2020, Flipkart undertook two more

acquisitions. Firstly, it acquired 100% stake in Scapic, a cloud-based platform which offered creation and publishing of augmented reality (AR) and 3D content (*Mint*, 2020c). The company had clients across e-commerce and marketing. The acquisition included the entire Scapic team of experienced developers and designers which would help Flipkart build deeper camera experiences and virtual storefronts, and bring new opportunities for brand advertising on its platform (Scapic). Secondly, Flipkart acquired the intellectual property of gaming start-up Mech Mocha and its gaming team (Flipkart Stories, 2022). Mech Mocha, which operates real-time multiplayer gaming app Hello Play, including ludo, carrom, cricket and other games, would allow Flipkart to enhance its gaming strategy as it looked to develop newer formats to boost user engagement on its own GameZone platform.

In April 2021, Flipkart entered the online travel booking sector by acquiring 100% ownership of Cleartrip, one of the oldest travel booking portals in India (ETech, 2021). Cleartrip was one of the first to incorporate product design that focussed on enhancing customer experience. The acquisition included Cleartrip employees, who had deep industry knowledge and technology capabilities and were expected to enable Flipkart Group to provide deeper value and travel experiences for its customers. However, Cleartrip would continue to operate as a separate brand and work closely with Flipkart to further develop technology solutions.

In July 2021, Flipkart launched Shopsy, an app that would enable anybody from anywhere in India to start their online business without any investment. With the ability to influence their local network and fulfil their aspirations, users of Shopsy would be able to share catalogues of a wide selection of 15 crore products offered by Flipkart sellers. These ranged across fashion, beauty, mobiles, electronics and home, reaching potential customers via popular social media and messaging apps. The objective was to enable over 25 million online entrepreneurs by 2023 as they reaped the benefits of digital commerce (Abrar, 2021). With this app, Flipkart opened up its years of e-commerce expertise to Indian entrepreneurs. Users can simply register on the Shopsy app using their phone numbers and begin their online entrepreneurial journey. Budding entrepreneurs can now set up their business as long as they have access to a network of people that trust them, without the hassle of investment, inventory or logistics management. This initiative is likely to boost new entrepreneurship and through them, Flipkart sales.

In July 2021, Flipkart raised an unprecedented amount of US$3.6 billion, one of the largest by any Indian start-up (Sarkar, 2021). This round of funding was led by GIC, Canada Pension Plan Investment Board (CPP Investments), SoftBank Vision Fund 2 and Walmart, along with investments from sovereign funds DisruptAD, Qatar Investment Authority, Khazanah Nasional Berhad, Tencent, Willoughby Capital, Antara Capital, Franklin Templeton and Tiger Global. The post-money valuation stood at US$37.6 billion. Together so far, Flipkart has raised nearly US$13 billion in around 25+ rounds (Walmart Press Release, 2021; Crunchbase).

In December 2021, Flipkart entered the healthcare sector by acquiring the online pharmacy and digital healthcare start-up, Sastasundar.com (Flipkart Press Release (FKH+) 2021). The new business vertical in the health sector would be known as Flipkart Health+. The objective was to provide quality and affordable healthcare through an e-pharmacy.

In January 2022, Flipkart's start-up accelerator Flipkart Leap deepened its engagement with the ecosystem. The accelerator evolved into two new programmes, namely Flipkart Leap Ahead (FLA) and Flipkart Leap Innovation Network (FLIN). FLA, under Flipkart Ventures, will invest in seed-stage start-ups which are innovative and working at the cutting edge of technologies with disruptive business models across sectors such as fintech, supply chain, SaaS, alternate commerce, B2B, sustainability and health. FLIN is designed to commercially engage with start-ups that have a viable product that would solve problems across themes such as: rethinking supply chain, building retail tech, accelerating digital commerce, future of fashion, and redefining customer experience (Flipkart Leap; Flipkart Ventures; Flipkart Press Release-Leap 2022).

In January 2022, Flipkart made one more acquisition, of electronics re-commerce company Yaantra, a brand that repairs and sells refurbished consumer tech products such as smartphones and laptops (Flipkart Press Release, 2022). This would help Flipkart to further strengthen its reverse supply chain and to enhance after-sales offerings for its smartphone customers as well as promote its refurbished goods sales.

In April 2022, Flipkart made its latest acquisition. It acquired ANS Commerce, a direct-to-consumer (D2C) software-as-a-service (SaaS) platform (Business Standard, 2022; IANS *Times of India*, 2022). ANS Commerce, founded in 2017, offers a variety of services to businesses and brands which are interested in selling online. As part of its services, it offers the creation of digital storefronts, integration with marketplaces, warehouse and facility management. Flipkart had a business relationship with ANS Commerce for its accelerator project Flipkart Leap, prior to the former's acquisition, for about one year.

In April 2022, Flipkart also marked its entry into the health sector by launching the Flipkart Health Plus App, a new platform that will onboard more than 500 independent sellers with a network of registered pharmacists for validation of medical prescriptions and accurate dispensation of medicines. The new platform will aim to serve more than 20,000 pin codes in the country (*The Economic Times*, 2022). The objective is to solve the critical gap of accessibility to genuine medicines and healthcare products and services across the country. In the immediate future, Flipkart Health Plus plans to diversify its offerings to tele-consultation and e-diagnostics, etc., to customers.

The chronology of events from May 2018 till April 2022 is briefly presented in Table 3.2. They broadly cover these aspects: the change in ownership and management, continued growth in terms of periodic fundraising, creation of new ventures and business vertical diversification, M&As, partnerships, process/market/financial innovations, co-investments and start-up promotion initiatives, apart from a steady increase in its valuation. It is important to note that today Flipkart is the most funded unicorn in India (*Venture Intelligence*, 2021) and an ace in the field of M&As in the country (*India Briefing*, 2022).

Table 3.2
Chronology of Events (from May 2018 to April 2022)

Year	Event
May 2018	Walmart acquires a major stake (77%) in Flipkart—as a result, Flipkart becomes part of a Fortune 500 US MNC
	Sachin Bansal, one of the co-founders, exits from the company
	Binny Bansal continues as a minority shareholder
August 2018	Launches 2GUD.com to sell certified refurbished goods, as its first-ever platform for selling refurbished goods
	M&A of Liv.ai., a speech recognition AI start-up
	Acquires Israel-based retail analytics company, Upstream Commerce
July 2019	Launches co-branded credit card with Axis Bank
	Launches own venture capital fund, Flipkart Ventures
	Launches Flipkart Samarth, an initiative to help unorganized/disadvantaged sectors with marketing
August 2019	Partners with Authentic Brands
November 2019	Acquires stake in EasyRewardz, a loyalty points management start-up
December 2019	Buys a minority stake in B2B logistics start-up Shadowfax
	Launches Flipkart Quick to deliver a select brand of products in 90 minutes

Year	Event
August 2020	Launches a start-up accelerator, Flipkart Leap Launches digital B2B platform Flipkart Wholesale to help small traders and MSMEs
November 2020	M&A of Scapic, a cloud-based platform, and IP of a gaming start-up, Mech Mocha.
April 2021	Acquires 100% stake in Cleartrip, an online travel start-up
July 2021	Launches Shopsy, an app to enable launching of online business by anybody from anywhere in India (to promote entrepreneurship)
November 2021	Acquires online pharmacy and digital healthcare start-up, Sastasundar.com
January 2022	Flipkart Leap is bifurcated into 'Flipkart Leap Ahead' to invest in seed-stage start-ups, and 'Flipkart Leap Innovation Network' to engage with mature start-ups
	Acquires electronic re-commerce start-up Yaantra
April 2022	Acquires ANS Commerce, a direct-to-consumer (D2C) software as a service (SaaS) platform
	Launches Flipkart Health Plus app

In the whole process of sustained growth, Flipkart has experienced periodic attrition of highly talented employees, like any other firm would experience. However, the uniqueness of this attrition is that many of its former executives have built tech start-ups by deploying their innovative ideas and investing their own savings as seed money. More than 200 such tech start-ups (https://inc42.com/features/flipkart-mafia/) have already emerged and continue to do so, led by former employees of Flipkart who are known as ex-Flipsters. This development could be considered a major contribution of Flipkart to the start-up ecosystem of India, among others. Eight of these tech start-ups such as PhonePe were later acquired by Flipkart. Thus, they have become a part of the M&As by Flipkart. Many ex-employees of Flipkart have joined other upcoming start-ups as employees. In addition, several Flipsters are involved in multiple tech start-ups across India as investors and mentors. This sums up the core activities of Flipkart since its inception till now.

Business Structure and Growth Performance of Flipkart

Against this backdrop, it is pertinent to examine the current business structure and growth performance of Flipkart. Since its origin, Flipkart has evolved to become a complex business structure comprising multiple entities and subsidiaries. Flipkart's Indian entities are owned by Flipkart Pvt Ltd registered in Singapore. The Singapore-registered entity is the main holding company under which there are many subsidiaries, major ones being Flipkart Myntra, PhonePe, Ekart, Flipkart Wholesale, Jeeves, Cleartrip and Flipkart Health Plus (Flipkart Corporate).

Flipkart has grown in terms of both employment and revenue, over the years. Starting with just two founders in 2007, it has steadily grown in terms of direct full-time employment to around 15,000 employees in 2022. Thus,

Flipkart employment has grown at an average rate of about 42.15% CAGR during 2009–2022. Flipkart's revenue stood at INR 4 crore/US$479,000 in 2009 (Hossan-*Business Inspection*, 2021), increasing to reach INR 7,308.1 crores/ US$875.1 million in 2014 (Jayadevan-*Factor Daily* [A], 2016). Revenue steadily increased since then to INR 15,403.3 crores/US$1.8 billion in 2016 (Jayadevan, *Factor Daily* [B], 2016), INR 19,854 crores/US$2.37 billion in 2017 (Khatri, *Inc42*, 2018), and exceeded INR 51,176 crores/US$6.1 billion in 2021–22 (*Onmanorama*, 2024). Flipkart's revenue grew at an average rate of about 106.98% CAGR from 2009 to 2022. It is against this backdrop that we need to analyse the strategy and achievements of Flipkart, its causal factors, and its implications for the firm as much as for the economy.

Table 3.3
Growth of Flipkart: Employment and Revenue during 2008-2022

Year	Employment (No.)	Total Revenue (Rs Crore)
2009	150	4
2014	7,000	7,308.1
2022	~15,000	51,176.00
CAGR	Employment (%)	Total Revenue (%)
2009–2022	**42.51**	**106.98**

*Sources: (Employment: Hossan-*Business Inspection*, 2021; IndiaTVNews, 2018;* The Economic Times*, 2014; NDTV Profit; PTI, 2023;* Business Standard *New Delhi, 2023)*

*(Revenue: Hossan-*Business Inspection*, 2021; Jayadevan-*Factor Daily*, 2016;* Onmanorama*, 2024)*

Flipkart Growth Strategy and Achievements: The Role of Corporate Entrepreneurship

Flipkart has emerged as an e-commerce tech start-up to meet the potential but unaddressed customer needs in the e-commerce industry of India, through technology. Therefore, customers remained the central focus of Flipkart's attention in all its subsequent initiatives. On the one hand, Flipkart created and developed its own supply capacity to serve the growing e-commerce market, and on the other, it contributed to a steady increase in demand through offering varied financial products and services and enabling customers' purchasing power. Thus, Flipkart has uniquely and simultaneously contributed to supply capability building and demand generation, and gained consistently for its growth, over the period from 2008 till 2022.

Given this, the following three questions are relevant:

1. How did Flipkart build its capabilities to steadily increase its product offerings, over time?
2. How did Flipkart diversify its business verticals as a means of growth over time?
3. How did Flipkart ensure a steady increase in demand for its ever-expanding product portfolios over time?

The first and foremost factor which was responsible for Flipkart's stupendous growth story was its founders and management, duly backed by its ownership and multiple investors. The single-minded focus and devotion to Indian customers, the customer-first approach (despite a change in management twice, and a change in ownership), has been the most outstanding feature of this growth story. To achieve the objective, the founders and management used both technology and strategy innovatively.

At the outset, the founders and management focussed on building internal capabilities in terms of decisive talent, and supply chain and logistics infrastructure for timely delivery of its products to customers. Audacity and aggressiveness have been the characteristics of this strategy from day one. It was realized at the beginning that 'building capability internally/organically' (in terms of infrastructure and talent) for a young firm would involve multiple challenges and consume time. Therefore, Flipkart's management decided to acquire and/or develop partnerships with complementary start-ups from its early days. Wherever talent was crucial, strategic M&As involved talent acquisition as well. Alternatively, where only IP was decisive, acquisition was confined to IPs excluding talent.

Thus, periodic M&As and partnerships became another key feature of management strategy to achieve its objective. (Flipkart was one of the unicorns in India to achieve the maximum number of M&As [22] since inception [Rath, 2022]). This was supplemented by raising much-needed finance periodically, which in turn facilitated M&As. Talent acquisition and accumulation enabled Flipkart to start its own new ventures and/or platforms within, though some of them failed to make a mark. Thus, founders/management tasted failure in their early days. But failure was a 'stepping stone to success' through hard learning. The successful new ventures contributed to infrastructure development as well as to carrying out of process innovations. Thus, talent acquisition and build-up, M&As and partnerships, and fundraising formed the base for three intermediate outcomes: building much-needed technology infrastructure including supply chain and logistics, process innovations, and market/financial innovations.

Talent is a fundamental requirement for any firm that intends to grow steadily by consistently meeting its customer needs. This assumes added significance in a technology-intensive sector such as e-commerce. Therefore, Flipkart management resorted to talent acquisition organically through direct recruitment by the management, as well as inorganically through periodic M&As. Periodic fundraising enabled both kinds of talent acquisitions. At the same time, the accumulated talent base of Flipkart, in turn, would have facilitated periodic fundraising.

However, talent acquisition and accumulation have a flip side as well, particularly in a tech start-up. Some of the well-trained tech talent is likely to leave for better opportunities in other firms or to set up their own start-ups, after gaining some amount of experience, exposure and confidence (apart from savings). Flipkart has experienced 'talent attrition' like any other firm in any industry. Many of the former executives (known as Flipsters) became entrepreneurs by initiating their own start-ups. Flipkart management soon realized the value of collaborating with those among them who provided complete technology solutions to customer-centric problems, and developed partnerships or subsequently acquired them.

M&As and partnerships can act as a massive growth engine but these would pose unique risks and challenges to any firm. The challenges largely pertain to identifying targets, determining the payment, and integrating these with the acquired firm. In fact, empirical evidence shows that globally about 70% to 90% of M&As fail (Christensen, et al., 2011). When a CEO wants to boost corporate performance or jump-start long-term growth, an M&A would appear extraordinarily seductive (Christensen, et al., 2011). In fact, M&As are designed to address multiple needs: to acquire talent and intellectual property, customers and product capabilities, to increase their total addressable market (TAM), to fill critical gaps in service offerings, to leverage synergies, to add a new business vertical, and to save time and long learning curves, among others (Livne, 2022). However, M&As can also be a disaster if not handled well, due to factors such as cultural clashes, cause for distraction for senior management, loss of brand strength, etc. Overall, M&As are an important means of corporate entrepreneurship for achieving consistent firm growth (King, et al., 2018).

Perhaps it is here that Flipkart has been highly successful. In its brief history of about one and half decades, Flipkart has audaciously acquired more than 22 start-ups (Rath, 2022). As a result, it has been able to strengthen its talent pool, IP and product capabilities, leading to early entry into new business verticals, apart from obtaining their customer base. Partnerships are primarily aimed at leveraging synergies for mutual benefit. Further, each M&A and/or co-investment or partnership would have invariably necessitated organizational restructuring while integrating the acquired start-up or while collaborating with the partners. Both would have led to further consolidating its technology infrastructure involving supply chain and logistics for meeting customer needs efficiently, apart from facilitating process innovations. Flipkart has successfully and competently handled all these issues.

The successive handling of strategic M&As, co-investments and business collaborations would have led to Flipkart's further visibility and reputation in the market, which in turn would have enabled periodic fundraising from VCs and other investors. It is important to note that while Flipkart has acquired more than 22 tech start-ups, it has raised nearly US$13 billion in around 25 rounds, since inception (Crunchbase; Rath 2022).

Through talent acquisition, M&As and partnerships, and periodic fundraising, Flipkart has innovatively adopted diverse elements of Industry 4.0. comprising:

- Digital payments
- Data analytics
- Artificial intelligence and machine learning
- Augmented reality
- The internet of things
- Digital mapping to strengthen supply logistics
- SaaS
- Promotion of digital start-ups, among others

Thus, over time, it has acquired the much-needed technological prowess to 'understand and meet customer needs' and cope with emerging challenges in the context of the Fourth Industrial Revolution.

To sum up, it is a talent acquisition-led talent base, M&As and partnerships, and fundraising which together enabled Flipkart to build its capabilities, in terms of technology infrastructure involving supply chain and logistics as well as process innovations. This has led to a steady diversification of its business verticals and increase its product categories from a single product at the time of inception to more than 80 by 2022. This explains how Flipkart has built its supply capabilities over time. Yet, that resolved only one side of the challenge for growth, that is, supply.

The other side of the challenge is demand generation. This had multiple dimensions including the following:

1. Understanding the market culture in terms of buying habits and buying power of Indian consumers
2. Winning consumer confidence at the outset, for online purchases and building on working any trust gaps for online purchases
3. Increasing the number of customers steadily by increasingly enabling the 'ease of purchasing', and meeting market aspirations of as many customers as possible, by helping them convert their 'desire' into 'demand'

This assumes significance in an emerging economy like India, for multiple reasons. Firstly, Indian consumers in general were comfortable buying consumer goods offline as they could see and obtain the products instantaneously once the payment was made. Secondly, India was known for its underdeveloped infrastructure for online purchase by customers as also for online sale by sellers. At that time, many fly-by-night online shopping portals were prevalent in the market, and many customers experienced failed orders or products not delivered on time and had broken online transaction experiences—all of which had fueled the customers' online shopping phobia. Thirdly, the consumer class in India is highly fragmented with a larger pool living in the lower middle income and low-income households where literacy level is relatively low and consumer desires are not likely to be backed by the necessary purchasing power for one-time payment, for both consumer durables and non-durables. Fourthly, given the low purchasing power of lower middle income and low-income households, they are accustomed to purchasing goods from local retailers, which has potential for garnering indirect demand as much as direct demand.

Given this, a steady increase in supply capability and product offerings will not lead to demand generation spontaneously. Flipkart founders/management understood these realities of the Indian market at the beginning itself. Therefore, innovative finance/market strategies to generate demand were introduced right after inception.

At the outset, winning consumer confidence was the priority. Therefore, for the first time ever, Flipkart introduced the 'cash on delivery' scheme in the Indian market. This was followed by a 30-day 'no questions asked' replacement policy. This would have significantly boosted the visibility and credibility of Flipkart in the nascent e-commerce industry in India, thereby contributing to demand generation. Subsequently, the innovative 'kids as adults' advertisement also helped boost Flipkart sales.

Secondly, certain M&As would have enabled Flipkart to

achieve twin objectives: to acquire the strength of such start-ups for efficient business diversification and to add the existing buyers of acquired start-ups of different business verticals to Flipkart's customer pool (i.e., market expansion).

Thirdly, understanding the buying behaviour of online customers and targeting them appropriately through personalized email notifications, facilitating their online purchases through exclusive apps, facilitating their payment options through an exclusive credit card and/or digital payments through PhonePe, etc., were measures to boost existing demand from tech-savvy customers. This is in addition to the Big Billion Days Sale aimed at the wider customer base to achieve spikes in sales.

Fourthly, to meet the aspirations of lower middle income and lower-income customers, Flipkart introduced several market/financial innovations to convert their desire (mere wish to have a commodity) into demand (desire backed by the necessary purchasing power). 'No cost EMI', 'EMI on debit cards', 'buy now, pay later', and entry and promotion of 'refurbished goods market' were initiatives that would have significantly transformed the 'desire' of consumers for hitherto unaffordable products into demand. This would have had a significant positive impact on demand generation.

Fifthly, making use of AI and AR for voice solutions in vernacular languages was a major step towards penetrating customer groups that were not fluent in using English for online transactions. This would enable Flipkart to further penetrate the 'hidden and unexplored demand' of customers who had stayed away due to language barriers.

Sixthly, the entry into B2B segment through an exclusive platform to connect local manufacturers, including micro, small and medium enterprises (MSMEs), with retailers and bringing the entire wholesale market at their fingertips, enabling the emergence of new entrepreneurship across the country through a separate app (Shopsy), helped generate indirect demand for Flipkart. At the same time, they would have contributed to the much-needed development of the MSME ecosystem as well.

Finally, by entering as many tech-related verticals as possible—such as books, electronics, grocery, games, courier, financial services, health, travel, lifestyle, and more—Flipkart was trying to capture the demand for those services from their existing customer base. Together, all these would have contributed to a steady increase in demand for Flipkart.

Thus, Flipkart has exhibited entrepreneurial culture successfully ever since its birth, involving strategic M&As, building talent in-house and through partnerships, raising funds to build technology infrastructure, implementing process/market/financial innovations, and thereby duly focussing on supply creation as much as demand generation. The simultaneous focus on supply and demand stands out as the unique feature of the corporate entrepreneurship model pursued by Flipkart. Altogether, this would have contributed to the accelerated growth of its revenue consistently over time.

The consistent revenue growth, in turn, would have contributed to building confidence in the founders/ management, enabled periodic fundraising and further talent acquisition and strategic M&As for building infrastructure, and carrying out process and market/financial innovations. Thus, Flipkart has developed a unique model of corporate entrepreneurship in the Indian start-up ecosystem, which has been succinctly presented in Figure 3.1. A brief description of the model is in order.

When an industry is underdeveloped in a developing economy, the challenges for steady growth of a start-up can be multifold. It is entirely different from entering an already developed industry with a definite demand base. In such already developed industries, product innovativeness with a strong dose of marketing is likely to enable the growth of a newly entered start-up. However, when a technology-intensive industry is hardly developed and does not have an established demand base, a start-up would face the challenges of developing/obtaining technology infrastructure and adequate/appropriate technology talent (human resources) for *supply*, and customers with adequate purchasing power for *demand*. This understanding would call for simultaneous focus of a start-up on supply and demand. This is precisely what the founders/management of Flipkart have done soon after its inception.

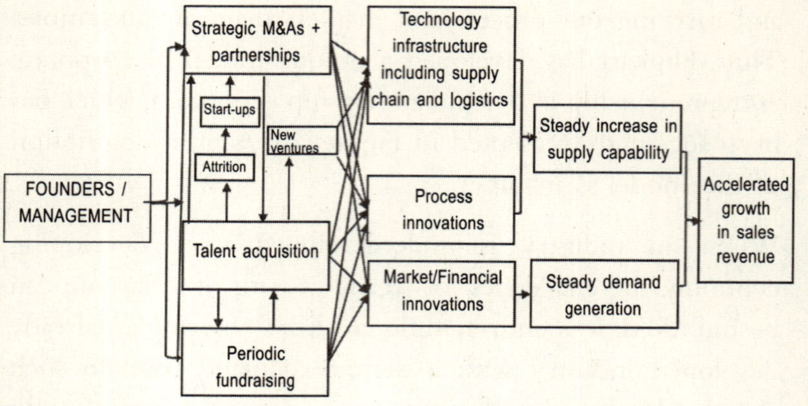

Figure 3.1: The growth of Flipkart from inception to internationalization: The role of corporate entrepreneurship

The founders and management of Flipkart focussed on talent building, fundraising and M&As, as well as partnerships, apart from creating new ventures internally, to build necessary technology infrastructure, and resorted to process innovations for a steady increase in supply, and finance and market innovations for a steady generation of demand. It is the success achieved on both fronts that enabled Flipkart to achieve unprecedented revenue growth in India's e-commerce industry.

In the process, Flipkart has also contributed to the development of an entrepreneurial ecosystem for start-ups, particularly in Bangalore. This deserves more description. Bangalore's entrepreneurial ecosystem can be defined as a nucleus surrounded by two outer layers and a triple helix base (Figure 3.2). The nucleus refers to prospective and functioning start-up founders [1]. The first outer layer consists of five indispensable components: namely finance

[2], marketing [3], human resources [4], support system comprising incubators and accelerators [5], and business and technology mentors [6]. The second outer layer comprises three supportive elements: namely culture [7], media [8] and weather [9]. The triple helix base includes government [10], industry [11] and academia [12], which directly or indirectly contributes to the generation of nucleus as well as indispensable and supportive components.

The arrows in the figure indicate constant interaction between the various components of the ecosystem for the generation of start-ups (Figure 3.2) (Bala Subrahmanya, 2021).

The entire ecosystem is focussed on or driven towards the generation and promotion of start-ups. That is why start-ups form the nucleus [1] of the ecosystem. The five indispensable factors are essential for an ecosystem to emerge, to survive, and be effective, whereas the secondary (supplementary) factors emerge and grow along with the growth of the ecosystem (Bala Subrahmanya, 2021). The founders of Flipkart as part of the nucleus [1] and Flipkart as a part of industry [11] have made significant contributions to the nurturing of Bangalore's start-up ecosystem (Figure 3.2). It has contributed to the strengthening of the nucleus as well as the five indispensable components and two of the three supplementary components of the ecosystem. Flipkart and its founders have directly provided finance, marketing support, mentoring support and support system (in the form of accelerators), and directly and indirectly provided support to the nucleus, human resources, culture and media, among others. This requires an elaboration.

Firstly, Flipkart has created many new ventures/platforms

within the company. These are 'internal start-ups' or 'start-ins'. An internal start-up is a separate business entity of an operating high-tech company (Nasheim, 2000). The employees in charge of such internal start-ups would have developed it from scratch and continue to operate as entrepreneurs. This would play an important role in creating entrepreneurship within the company. Equally importantly, many former employees who have left Flipkart have created their own start-ups outside. Some of the new ventures/platforms/units created by Flipkart were Flipkart Logistics (which later became Ekart), Flipkart Payment Gateway Services, AIforIndia, 2GUD.com, Flipkart Wholesale and Shopsy.

Most of these entities exist and operate today as part of Flipkart. More importantly, according to estimates, by 2017 about 233 Flipsters (former Flipkart employees) have created more than 207 start-ups (mostly in Bangalore) (Sareen, 2017). Some of these start-ups have become unicorns themselves, whereas about 59 start-ups have discontinued and exited from the market. This implies that about 71% of the Flipsters-initiated start-ups are surviving and/or growing. This is unprecedented even by global standard because globally 90% of start-ups fail (Howarth, 2022). In the process, Flipkart and Flipsters would have become a 'role model' and thereby led to the emergence of many prospective start-up founders in the city. Thus, the founders and Flipkart have significantly contributed to the generation of the nucleus [1] of Bangalore's entrepreneurial ecosystem.

Secondly, it has contributed considerably to the five indispensable components, namely finance, marketing, human resources, support system and mentors. Flipkart has co-invested in many start-ups such as Jeeves Consumer Services Private Limited (later fully acquired) (Flipkart Stories), Wehive Technologies (Dalal, *Mint*, 2022), Zinka (Flipkart Stories, Flipkart Corporate), MapmyIndia, TinyStep, EasyRewardz (EazyRewardz Corp), and Shadowfax, among others. In addition, Flipkart founders, its senior executives and Flipsters have invested in many more start-ups at various stages. In 2019, Flipkart formally launched its own investment arm, Flipkart Ventures, to invest in early-stage ventures. This explains how Flipkart has become a source of finance [2] for the start-up ecosystem.

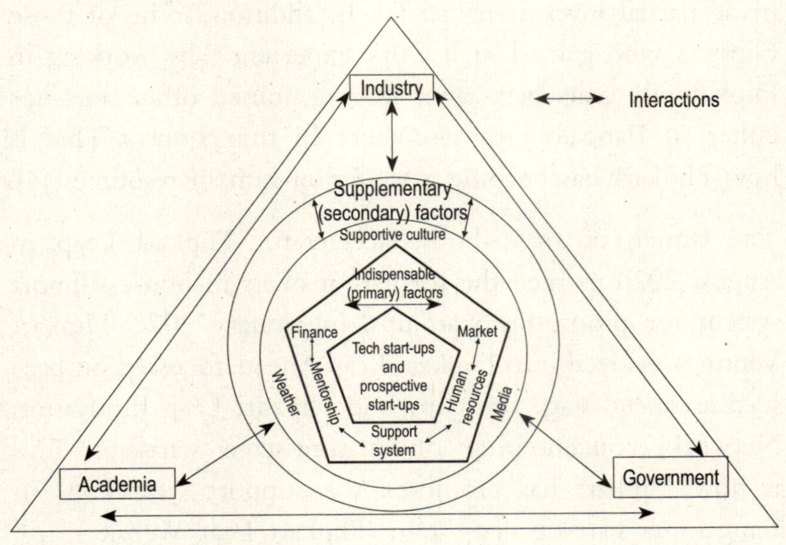

Figure 3.2: Entrepreneurial ecosystem for start-ups in Bangalore: Structure, components and relative importance

Source: Bala Subrahmanya (2021)

Flipkart has provided marketing support to start-ups at different stages of its lifecycle. In all the co-invested start-ups referred to above, Flipkart developed business collaborations. More importantly, Flipkart provided exit option to many start-up founders through M&As. Since its inception and over 15 years, it has acquired 22 start-ups, which were operating at different stages of their lifecycles (both successful and failed ones) (Rath, 2022). That is how Flipkart has become a source of market support [3].

Flipkart has rendered direct human resource support to all those start-ups that it acquired or start-ups in which it has made partial investments so far. In addition, some of those Flipsters who gained 'rich work experience' by working in Flipkart for years have, after leaving, joined other start-ups either in Bangalore or elsewhere in the country. That is how Flipkart has become a source of human resources [4].

The launch of an in-house accelerator, Flipkart Leap, in August 2020 marked the formation of its in-house support system for promoting start-ups. In January 2022, Flipkart Ventures evolved into Flipkart Leap Ahead, focussed on pre-seed and seed-stage start-ups, and Flipkart Leap Innovation Network, concentrating on mature-stage start-ups. This is how Flipkart has promoted the support system [5] in Bangalore's start-up ecosystem (Flipkart Leap Website).

Apart from Flipkart's founders, many of its employees, particularly senior executives who have technology and business experience, have been mentoring multiple start-ups in Bangalore and outside, wherever they have invested, along with their job responsibilities. Even ex-Flipsters who have become angel investors provide technology/

business mentoring to start-ups in which they have made investments. Thus, Flipkart is a source of mentorship [6] as well. This would have played a decisive role in developing product-market-fit (PMF) for many infant start-ups, not just in Bangalore but all across the country.

Flipkart's contribution is not confined to the nucleus and indispensable components of the ecosystem. Its multifold achievements have been nurturing the entrepreneurial culture [7] both within and outside Flipkart, not only in Bangalore but beyond the city as well. In fact, Flipkart's entrepreneurial culture itself would have been responsible for many Flipsters leaving the company and subsequently setting up their own start-ups. Similarly, Flipkart's direct and indirect achievements have been attracting media [8] attention regularly, which in turn contributes to the promotion of start-up culture and entrepreneurial ambition in the community at large. Thus, Flipkart has emerged as an ecosystem for start-ups by itself within the Bangalore start-up ecosystem. This sums up the ecosystem contributions of Flipkart (Figure 3.2).

Summary

Flipkart has been one of the most successful tech start-ups in India's start-up ecosystem. Since its birth in October 2007, it has come a long way. Its success is not confined to just firm-level performance but, more importantly, has had a significant impact on the entire ecosystem, India in general and, Bangalore in particular. The predominant factor behind the successful contributions of Flipkart has been the consistent entrepreneurial zeal of its founders/

management focussing on the customer, and pursuing strategic M&As, talent acquisition and periodic fundraising as the primary means of building technology infrastructure (including supply chain and logistics), process innovations and market/financial innovations. Though they have created new ventures within the organization, these have played a complementary role to their strategic M&As, and together played a role in promoting process innovations and technology infrastructure.

A steady development of technology infrastructure and process innovations enabled a steady increase in supply. On the other hand, a steady stream of market and financial innovations generated much-needed demand. Thus, it is the simultaneous push given to supply creation and demand generation that enabled Flipkart to register an unprecedented growth out of Bangalore. Thereby, Flipkart has developed a unique model of corporate entrepreneurship in Indian business. But that explains only one side of its achievements.

The other but equally impressive side of its achievements is its contribution to the development of the entrepreneurial ecosystem for start-ups in Bangalore and beyond. In the process of its own growth, Flipkart has not only generated multiple new ventures but also become a direct source of hundreds of start-ups by its former employees. Apart from its direct generation of start-up entrepreneurs, Flipkart provided the much-needed sources of indispensable components of an entrepreneurial ecosystem, namely finance, marketing, human resources, mentoring and a formal support system in the form of an accelerator. In addition, it nurtured the supportive components, namely entrepreneurial culture and media. It is these firm-level achievements and ecosystem-level contributions that make Flipkart unique and stand apart in the Indian start-up ecosystem.

4

ENTREPRENEURIAL CULTURE IN FLIPKART: KEY FEATURES AND OUTCOMES

Introduction

In the course of its remarkable growth, Flipkart has acquired several start-ups through M&As and backed and invested in several others. The exit of ex-Flipsters has led to the creation of hundreds of start-ups outside the company. Flipkart has acquired some of the start-ups created by ex-Flipsters, developed business relationships with others, while some have functioned independently and made a mark on their own. Some of the start-ups created by ex-Flipsters, such as PhonePe (which was later acquired by Flipkart but continues to function independently) and Udaan, have become unicorns in themselves.

This leads to three important questions:

1. Does Flipkart nurture an entrepreneurial culture within the organization? If yes, how?
2. Does the entrepreneurial culture nurtured within prompt Flipkart to resort to M&As, and support many other start-ups outside through investments and mentorship, among others?
3. Why could Flipkart contribute so many start-ups to the Indian start-up ecosystem in its brief history?

To answer these questions, we met Flipkart CEO Kalyan Krishnamurthy, co-founder and a member of the Board of Directors of Flipkart Binny Bansal, who was also founder COO and later worked as CEO for a brief period, 15 tenured senior executives, and founders of six acquired start-ups within Flipkart. In addition, we interviewed 22 ex-Flipsters who founded their own start-ups and continue to run them. This chapter analyses the questions raised above—based on primary data gathered through personal interviews—in the context of entrepreneurial culture.

Entrepreneurial Culture: Role and Importance

It is well understood that Flipkart founders/management have successfully acquired talented workforce, organically as well as inorganically, and resorted to periodic M&As and fundraising, which together enabled them to build the much-needed technology infrastructure and carry out process/market/financial innovations, apart from internally initiating new ventures. This led Flipkart to consistently build supply capability as well as generate demand, culminating in its phenomenal growth over the period. Thus, Flipkart has developed a unique model of corporate entrepreneurship and consistently gained out of it. But all this would not have been possible without a culture of entrepreneurship prevailing within the organization. It is the entrepreneurial culture which would have facilitated internal new ventures and innovations, as well as generated entrepreneurship for new ventures externally (by ex-Flipsters). This is because entrepreneurial culture has an important influence on corporate entrepreneurship (Turro, et al., 2014).

An entrepreneurial organizational culture can be defined as one in which new ideas and creativity are expected, experiments and risk-taking are encouraged, failure is tolerated, learning is promoted, product and process innovations are championed, and continuous change is viewed as a conveyor of opportunities (Ireland, et al., 2003). Thus, an entrepreneurial organizational culture can be defined as a culmination of these behavioural norms and cognitions shared by organizational employees (Shephered, Patzelt and Haynie, 2010). Though there are multiple definitions of entrepreneurial culture, there are some commonalities as they lay emphasis on pursuing change, innovation, risk-taking and opportunities.

Entrepreneurial culture is generally pursued because of its positive relationship with firm growth, firm performance, and success. Therefore, firms of all sizes need entrepreneurial behaviour to survive and perform in a competitive environment (Barringer and Bluedorn, 1999). Sometimes, it is extremely difficult to repeat the brilliant entrepreneurial success achieved at the beginning by the start-up founders. But if a growing firm has to succeed in the long run, there is a constant need to develop an entrepreneurial spirit and innovative climate at all organizational levels, from the top management team to each individual employee at the operational levels. An entrepreneurial firm focussed on employees creates a sense of belonging to an organization (Paunovic and Dima, 2014).

The most successful organizations build a culture that welcomes change as an opportunity, and does not view it as a threat (Lockhead, 2008). Challenging the status quo and encountering failures through the risk-taking process, but without severe punishment and penalty, represent an important value of the entrepreneurial culture. Entrepreneurial culture tolerates risk-taking and empowers employees to undertake calculated risks and to manage these efficiently. Open communication and high-quality teamwork are other important elements of entrepreneurial culture. At the same time, commitment to work and a sense of belonging to a particular organization are probably the determinants of entrepreneurial culture (Paunovic and Dima, 2014).

According to Russell and Russell (1992), innovation is at the heart of a firm's entrepreneurial culture, and it has certain essential characteristics, such as value for innovation as a practice and a source of competitive advantage, a focus on creativity and creative pursuits on the part of organizational members, resource support for creativity and innovation, information sharing among members, risk-taking and tolerance for failure, open-mindedness toward new ideas and initiatives, and a culture embracing implementation of innovation in all forms and at all levels of the organization. Chandler et al. (2000) contend that entrepreneurial culture is enhanced when employees trust and perceive support from a firm's management, the organizational system rewards innovation, and excessive work pressure that tends to stifle individual and team creativity is minimized.

A firm with an entrepreneurial culture innovates audaciously and regularly, is proactive, and assumes risks to carry out strategies to develop innovative products, services or processes (Lee and Peterson, 2000). Entrepreneurial culture includes risk-taking, putting up with failure, dealing with uncertain environments, pursuing opportunities, embracing flexibility, and creating an internal environment conducive to innovation (Hamel, 2002; Genc, 2012). It promotes new ideas, enables experimenting, and generates solutions to problems that ultimately contributes to organizational innovativeness (Lee and Peterson, 2000). Firms that engage in promoting entrepreneurial culture will experience positive outcomes in the form of new technologies, products, services and processes, which will ultimately enhance firm performance.

To develop an entrepreneurial culture within a growing firm, it is essential to develop appropriate systems of motivation, intangible as well as tangible, for its employees. Intangible systems to stimulate employees would include assigning autonomy, opportunities for personal advancement, more responsibilities, new challenges, pleasant work environment, flexible working hours, and so on. Tangible systems of motivation comprise awarding exceptional commitment and loyalty of employees at all management levels through higher salaries, bonuses and distribution of profits, among others. Top management has to build management teams who think more like entrepreneurs and not as professional managers, as a result of which entrepreneurial behaviour becomes one of the crucial dimensions of revitalization in a firm. Firms that consciously nurture entrepreneurial culture within their organizations and among employees stand to gain and succeed in the long run in their business performance (Paunovic and Dima, 2014).

The above discussion brings out some of the salient features of a firm that nurtures or pursues entrepreneurial culture, which are listed in Table 4.1. A firm that nurtures entrepreneurial culture will encourage its employees to continuously learn new things, experiment, challenge the status quo, welcome new ideas, initiatives and creativity, be proactive, take calculated risks, and implement innovations, while tolerating failure. This will be done by providing required resources at all times. Overall, this will go a long way towards boosting the morale of the talented workforce, helping develop a sense of commitment to the organization. The cumulative outcome of these efforts will be new initiatives and innovations for the benefit of the organization in the short run as much as in the long run. Given this, it is appropriate to understand how far Flipkart has imbibed these features within the organization and within its employees, and what the outcomes are.

Table 4.1
Salient Features of Entrepreneurial Culture of a Firm

Sl No.	Salient Features
1	Autonomy to its employees in functioning
2	Challenging the status quo
3	Continuous learning
4	Creating an environment conducive to innovation
5	Employee empowerment
6	Enabling experiments
7	Generating solutions to problems
8	Open-mindedness about new ideas, creativity and initiatives
9	Innovations in all forms and rewarding the successful ones
10	Proactiveness
11	Risk-taking
12	Resource support
13	Sense of belonging to the organization
14	Teamwork
15	Tolerance of failure
16	Work pressure is minimized

Entrepreneurial culture has to be initiated by the management and supported by senior/middle-level management executives. It will be reflected in the employees including entrepreneurs and those who have joined Flipkart through M&As. Further, it will be reflected by those Flipsters who have left the organization for creating their own start-ups.

Against this backdrop, we interviewed one of the co-founders of Flipkart, Binny Bansal, who has been associated with the company right from its inception, shouldering different responsibilities over a period of time—as one of the owners, as a former COO, as a former CEO, and as a director and shareholder (YourStory-Binny Bansal). We also interviewed current CEO Kalyan Krishnamurthy (LinkedIn-Kalyan Krishnamurthy), who was with Flipkart from 2010 to 2014 as CFO as well as one of the directors, and since 2017 has been its CEO (Chanchani-ET CIO, 2017). We interviewed 15 tenured senior/middle-level executives (including two intrapreneurs) and six founders of acquired start-ups who are now Flipkart employees. In addition, we interviewed 22 ex-Flipsters who are founders of start-ups currently operating outside Flipkart. Together they could reflect on the salient features of the entrepreneurial culture nurtured and prevalent at Flipkart, and its resultant benefits.

Entrepreneurial Culture in Flipkart

We have presented the perspectives on entrepreneurial culture as perceived by the founder and CEO, senior/middle level executives, founders of acquired start-ups, and ex-Flipsters who are founders and operators of start-ups outside Flipkart. Based on these multiple perspectives, we have analysed the entrepreneurial culture in Flipkart and its outcomes.

Founder/Management perspective

The origin of entrepreneurial culture in Flipkart can be traced to its 'Vision & Mission', which lays exclusive emphasis on 'meeting Indian customer needs across the length and breadth of the country through the provision of high-quality products at a reasonable price, through technology.' The vision and mission have remained the same since the beginning, though their articulation has been refined from time to time.

Towards this end, employees are recruited based on their talent and capability to perform, rather than solely on their qualifications and work experience. Employees are encouraged to think big and to think constantly to challenge the status quo, and given full responsibility for calculated risk-taking with adequate resources. Customer obsession is emphasised, audacious goals are set, and employees are held accountable, though failure is tolerated and not penalized. Employees are advised 'not to hesitate to take risks because of failure.' Importance is given to performance and capability, and not job experience. Emphasis is laid on quick decision-making and agility, and success is rewarded. Product development and innovations are constantly encouraged.

It was realized early that when an organization is structured and grown organically, its risk appetite is likely to decline gradually. To avoid this, employees are rotated between jobs and departments periodically. As a result, organizational restructuring occurs regularly; it has also evolved due to new business verticals and technology development, apart from dynamic business perspectives. This has enabled the organization to achieve 'structured risk-taking' with full knowledge of its pros and cons.

Given the above, Flipkart has adopted a novel approach to innovation. Innovation is solving an unsolved problem in a sustainable way, for the benefit of customers. Problems that are not yet solved in the Indian context are taken up and identified by either employees or management, or both. Thus, both bottom-up and top-down approaches are adopted for innovation. Innovation also enables customers to think radically differently for purchases. Accordingly, innovations may be process-, market- or finance-related, with the ultimate beneficiary being the customer.

Organizational restructuring and innovations are also facilitated by the periodic M&As done by Flipkart. The major objective of M&As is to acquire assets, capabilities and talent, and thereby achieve business vertical diversification. Start-ups with a similar culture, irrespective of whether they are successful or failed, are acquired. As part of the strategy, Flipkart has always acquired early-stage start-ups, since acquiring late-stage start-ups can be expensive, time-consuming and more challenging in terms of adapting.

Finally, it is the culture imbibed and experience gained at Flipkart (in terms of job profiles and decision-making) and the talent of the employees which have contributed to the start-ups founded by Flipsters, after their exit from Flipkart. The management has neither encouraged nor discouraged their employees to exit and create their own start-ups. Some of these start-ups, like PhonePe, were subsequently acquired by Flipkart. Thus, entrepreneurship by ex-Flipsters has proved beneficial to Flipkart in achieving its business vertical diversification.

However, Flipkart has not intentionally pursued corporate entrepreneurship comprising strategic renewal (involving periodic organization restructuring), M&As and innovations.

Rather, it has emerged out of learning and experience, over time. This could be why the corporate entrepreneurship model observed at Flipkart (as concluded in the previous chapter) is unique by any standard.

Perspectives of Flipkart executives and founders of acquired start-ups

The executives, by and large, were impressed with the vision and mission of Flipkart, which laid emphasis on 'transforming commerce through technology' and 'changing the shopping culture of Indians through technology'. Given this, without exception, these employees agree that organizational restructuring is a regular exercise done at Flipkart, and it has contributed to improving efficiency. Reorganization has also been due to scale expansion-led growth and new business verticals. Further, organizational restructuring is done regularly at Flipkart to energize and continuously help employees learn new things. Given this, a majority concluded that organizational restructuring, done for whatever reasons, has helped them in some contexts whereas adversely affected them in some other contexts.

The innovation culture in Flipkart stems from its obsession with its customers, and is primarily owed to its audacious growth plans. Empowering employees with trust played a major role in innovation. Bold goals and support to employees with resources to achieve those goals also played a role in innovation. The assignment of clear goals to employees without a clearly defined path prompted innovation by them. Employees are given autonomy to take up a problem for a complete solution and scale it up from ground zero. Thus, igniting curiosity with empowerment, challenging the status quo, allowing experimentation and keeping high trust in employees enabled them to carry out successful innovations. In all these, tolerating failure without penalty acted as a safety net, thereby boosting the employees' confidence in innovations. Experiments are encouraged and if they are not successful, quick failures are recommended and such experiments are aborted.

Fast and democratic decision making, and limited bureaucracy are the hallmarks of Flipkart, which also facilitates innovations. Flipkart has innovated across digital platforms, fintech, its B2C brand, cash on delivery, and more. Risk-taking and innovation are considered the backbone of Flipkart today. Innovations built confidence to solve new problems and brought visibility to many of these executives. It led to intellectually stimulating learning and higher motivation. This has enabled further innovations at Flipkart, creating a platform to think bigger.

It is the hunger for growth which has been leading Flipkart to continuously diversify its business, while understanding customer needs constantly helps it achieve diversification. Ultimately, the goal is to make Flipkart a one-stop shop for all kinds of e-commerce in India. In the process, it has enabled employees to put forth their ideas, develop proposals, choose a team within Flipkart, understand the context and strategize, keep iterating, and successfully implement the project. It is the inherent need to do new things continuously that drives business vertical diversification, whose ultimate aim is achieving customer satisfaction.

Organizational restructuring, innovation and business

vertical diversification are the components of corporate entrepreneurship, and together they have contributed to the remarkable growth of Flipkart. But all these have been facilitated by the talented employees of Flipkart, who have been given complete freedom in decision making and implementation. Performers are rewarded. Thus, identifying the right people and assigning the right tasks enabled Flipkart to achieve accelerated growth, via organizational restructuring, innovation and business vertical diversification.

Given the above, Flipkart has multiple objectives in periodically going for M&As, used as a means of acquiring talent, capability, technology, and entering into a new business vertical, apart from adding new customers. Developing a new technology or capability requires time, talent and resources. If a start-up has all of these, and if Flipkart observes it has compatibility with the former, acquisition appears as the best strategy, as it saves time and resources, apart from getting talent and capability for the acquired company. For the founders of acquired start-ups, it is an opportunity to understand how to scale up, become a better leader and solve problems completely and holistically (from the beginning till the end). These learnings reenergize their entrepreneurial spirit.

Perspectives of ex-Flipsters as founders of start-ups

In the process of accelerated growth, Flipkart has experienced attrition of talented employees, many of whom founded their own start-ups. Ex-Flipsters who founded their own start-ups have gradually and steadily gained visibility. Among other factors, financial security and professional confidence gained at Flipkart have contributed to the emergence of many ex-Flipsters as start-up founders. Flipkart has always encouraged people to experiment within the company by giving autonomy to individuals and teams. Flipkart also emphasises an entrepreneurial mindset while hiring talent, giving responsibilities and freedom to encourage the entrepreneurial spirit. They continuously question the status quo and practise customer-oriented thinking with the use of technology, prompting an ambitious entrepreneurial approach. Overall, Flipkart has become a fertile ground for entrepreneurship.

While at Flipkart many of them were exposed to fundraising, adding to their confidence. Further, they had the opportunity of carrying out assignments with ownership. Decision-making at Flipkart is quick; it involves both top-down and bottom-up approaches. Flipkart provides ample scope for employees to learn risk-taking and problem solving, the much-needed virtues of entrepreneurship. As a result, many work within Flipkart as independent executives, and have acquired the capability to conceptualize, ideate and develop a product for a suitable market.

Thus, the freedom to think and act, along with the assigned responsibility, has enabled many a Flipster to leave the company to experiment with their own start-ups and if they failed, they would attempt to return to other well-established start-ups like Flipkart, overall boosting the confidence to go out and experiment. The fact that they had worked at Flipkart and obtained the experience of founding a start-up acts as an 'additional qualification' to get accepted in the ecosystem for re-employment. Further, many of them gained from the Flipkart brand name, after exiting and while setting up their own start-ups, for obtaining funds, mentorship, talent hiring, etc.

The series of successful start-ups emerging from Flipsters would motivate many more to think along the lines of becoming entrepreneurs on their own in the future. Overall, the start-ups of ex-Flipsters have proved beneficial to Flipkart as well, since the latter developed business relationships with some of them and went about acquiring others—for entering into a new business vertical, or acquiring capability, technology and talent, among others.

The Emergence of Entrepreneurial Culture in Flipkart: Inferences

Firms that can nurture a culture that is truly entrepreneurial provide themselves with a strong competitive advantage. They continuously look for opportunities to become competitive and grow faster. A firm is entrepreneurial if it has nurtured the skills and the mindset to drive innovation, problem-solving, creativity and intelligent and calculated risk-taking. Entrepreneurial firms empower such employees and teams for independent decision-making. Audacious goals are given to employees with resources for implementation. An entrepreneurial culture amplifies both organic growth and inorganic growth (through M&As). An entrepreneurial firm is customer-centric, aims at providing the best experiences for its customers, and takes direct ownership for customer satisfaction.

When an entrepreneurial firm acquires a new firm, it also acquires the latter's entrepreneurs and talent who enabled the acquired firm to reach the status of being a worthy acquisition. The entrepreneurial firm also creates a conducive environment for acquired entrepreneurs to thrive and fruitfully utilize their experience and talent. In the process, it amplifies the entrepreneurial potential of the acquired entrepreneurs. The above qualities of entrepreneurial culture are profoundly reflected in the convergence of perspectives revealed by the CEO of Flipkart, co-founder and one of the members of Board of Directors, senior/middle-level executives (including intrapreneurs), founders of acquired start-ups who are Flipsters currently, and ex-Flipsters who are founders of start-ups operating outside of Flipkart. The converged perspectives of entrepreneurial culture are presented in Table 4.2.

Table 4.2
Converged Perspectives on 'Entrepreneurial Culture in Flipkart': Data Triangulation

Perspective elements	Co-founder & CEO	Senior/ Middle-level executives and founders of acquired start-ups	Ex-Flipsters who are founders of start-ups outside of Flipkart
Agility/quick decision-making	√	√	√
Audacious goals	√	√	√
Autonomy to individuals and teams	√	√	√

Perspective elements	Co-founder & CEO	Senior/ Middle-level executives and founders of acquired start-ups	Ex-Flipsters who are founders of start-ups outside of Flipkart
Bottom-up and top-down approach for innovations	√	√	√
Challenging the status quo	√	√	√
Customer focus/ obsession	√	√	√
Empowering employees with trust	√	√	√
Employees encouraged to learn new things and do problem solving	√	√	√
Experiments encouraged	√	√	√
Failure tolerated and not penalized	√	√	
Innovations: Process/market/ finance	√	√	
Limited bureaucracy	√	√	

Perspective elements	Co-founder & CEO	Senior/ Middle-level executives and founders of acquired start-ups	Ex-Flipsters who are founders of start-ups outside of Flipkart
M&As for acquiring assets, technology, talent and entry into new business vertical	√	√	
Risk-taking encouraged	√	√	√
Supporting employees with resources	√	√	

Note: (√) indicates identification of a perspective

This convergence has significance because the founder and CEO represent ownership and management, while executives and founders of acquired start-ups represent the current employees, whereas founders of start-ups outside of Flipkart represent ex-employees of Flipkart. Thus, there is triangulation of three different data sources used to understand the presence and characteristics of entrepreneurial culture in Flipkart.

The term 'triangulation' refers to the practice of using multiple sources of data or multiple approaches for analysing data to enhance the credibility of a research study (Saikind, 2010). Triangulation has the advantage of overcoming the potential bias resulting from the use of a single method or a single source of data in a study (Nguyen, 2009). Triangulation is a foremost consideration in many qualitative research works. It is an attempt to gain more than one perspective on what is being investigated (Zeegers and Barron, 2015). Triangulation has three main merits: namely, it enhances validity and reliability, it creates a more comprehensive picture of a research problem, and it facilitates adoption of different ways of understanding a research problem (Nightingale, 2020). The data triangulation identifying the causes, key features and outcomes of entrepreneurial culture is presented in Figure 4.1.

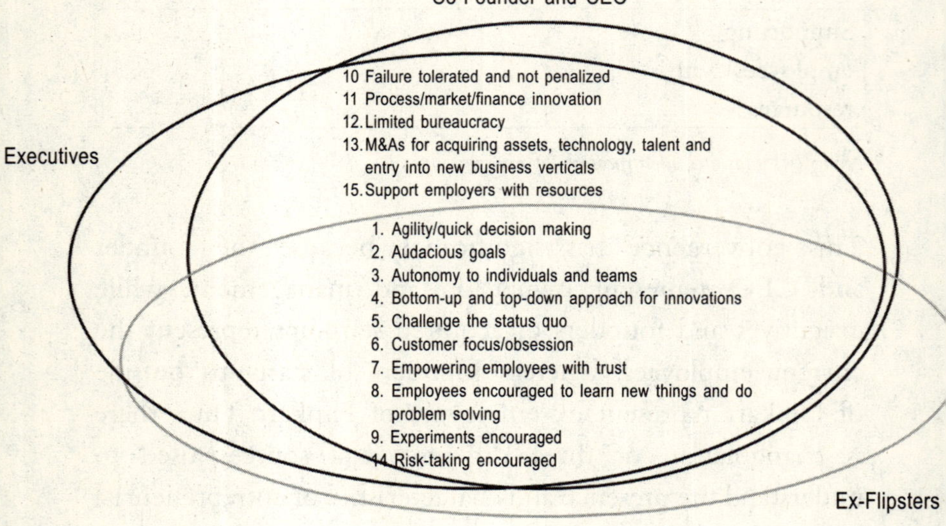

Figure 4.1: Entrepreneurial culture in Flipkart: Causes, features and outcomes

Based on the converged perspectives, entrepreneurial culture and its outcomes can be interpreted as follows:

1. The customer obsession and audacious goals have made the management set a high entry barrier for recruitment of technology/techno-managerial talent into Flipkart.
2. The employees and employee teams are given complete autonomy with assignments and resource support for risk-taking, and are encouraged to do experiments and challenge the status quo.
3. Thus, employees are adequately empowered to learn new things, identify problems and provide solutions.
4. New ideas/challenges may emerge from the top or from the bottom, for implementation.
5. In the process, decision-making is quick with limited bureaucracy, and failure is tolerated, without penalty.
6. Such an entrepreneurial environment (along with technology infrastructure comprising supply chain and logistics, and periodic fundraising) generates process/market/financial innovations.
7. Such an entrepreneurial environment will experience 'entrepreneurship eruptions' through exit of talented and ambitious employees to launch their own start-ups.
8. Such an entrepreneurial environment will attract early-stage start-ups for M&As, including the start-ups of ex-Flipsters, which would facilitate entry into new business verticals, technology and talent acquisition, apart from market amalgamation.
9. M&As of start-ups would further facilitate process/market/financial innovations.

10. The overall outcomes are a steady increase in supply as well as in demand, for an accelerated growth of the company.

This is presented in the form of a process flow diagram (PFD) in Figure 4.2. PFD is a graphical way of describing a process, its constituent tasks, and their sequence (Elahi, 2018). A PFD is a visual representation of the sequence of steps and decisions needed to perform a process. Each step in the sequence is noted within a diagram shape. Steps are linked by connecting lines and directional arrows. This allows anyone to view the PFD and logically follow the process from the beginning to the end.

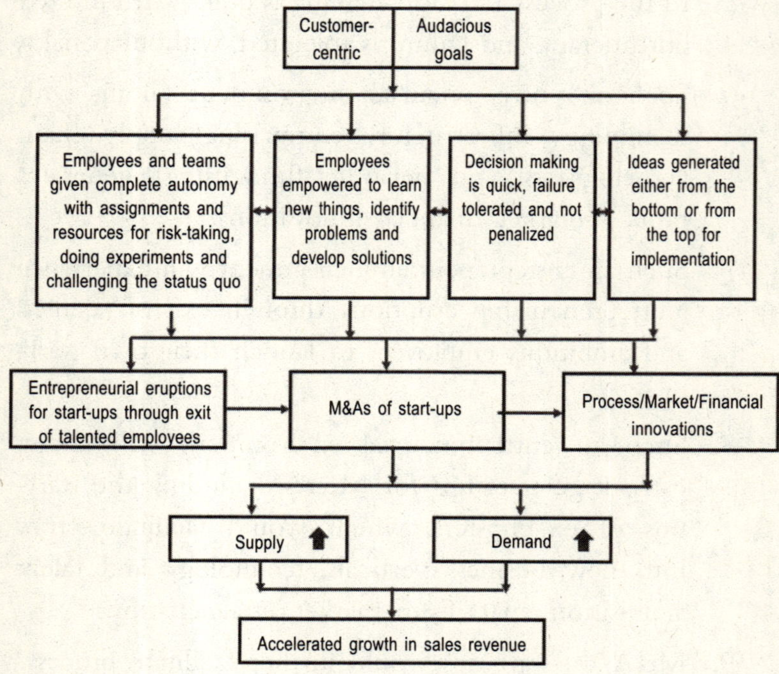

Figure 4.2: Process flow diagram of entrepreneurial culture in Flipkart: Causes, features and outcomes

The PFD has identified the causes and features of entrepreneurial culture, and its intermediate and final outcomes. The customer-centric focus and ambition to grow big has prompted the founders and the management to pursue entrepreneurial culture right after the inception of Flipkart and that has continued since then. The successful pursuit of entrepreneurial culture, which led to M&As of start-ups including some of the start-ups created by ex-Flipsters, led to process/market/financial innovations. The steady building up of infrastructure and raising of funds enabled M&As and innovations, which, in turn, contributed to further strengthening and development of infrastructure. Together they led to a steady increase in supply capability and demand generation, resulting in an accelerated growth of the company.

Summary

Flipkart founders had a single-minded focus on Indian customers, with the objective of transforming commerce through technology and thereby grow big, right after its inception. It was realized that this objective would be attainable only with a talented and highly motivated workforce and adequate and appropriate infrastructure, apart from finance. Therefore, employees were recruited based on talent and motivation rather than mere work experience. Employees were assigned tasks to be performed with full autonomy and accountability. They were assigned newer tasks through shifting job responsibilities and departments on a regular basis. This enabled them to constantly learn new things.

New ideas and risk-taking were encouraged, and required resources were provided. Employees were encouraged to conceptualize and implement projects with independence. This led to their empowerment, encouraged teamwork, and created within them a sense of belonging to their organization. This, in turn, led to technological innovations for infrastructure development (involving supply chain and logistics) and market/financial innovations for market development. Unsuccessful projects were allowed to fail quickly and aborted. Thus, quicker failures were encouraged but not penalized.

To achieve growth objectives, Flipkart's management resorted to M&As that enabled quicker business vertical diversification, technology and talent acquisitions, and market enlargement, apart from facilitating periodic fundraising. Periodic fundraising and talent acquisition would have facilitated M&As in turn. Thus, entrepreneurial culture has been nurtured in Flipkart right from the beginning. It is the entrepreneurial culture exhibited by the founders/management, and imbibed by employees (both directly recruited and acquired through M&As), which laid the foundation for pursuing corporate entrepreneurship in Flipkart. At the same time, Flipkart also experienced a steady attrition of entrepreneurial talent which led to the emergence of ex-Flipsters as entrepreneurs, leading to a series of start-ups, angels, mentors, etc., outside of it.

Talented and motivated employees, internal new ventures and M&As, apart from fundraising, enabled the company to continuously undertake process/market/financial innovations and build technology infrastructure involving supply chain and logistics. Infrastructure development and process innovations led to a steady increase in supply capability, whereas market/financial innovations generated the much-needed demand. A steady increase in supply and demand together led Flipkart to achieve a remarkable growth, from its inception to reach the stage of internationalization.

5

CURRENT STATUS OF CORPORATE ENTREPRENEURSHIP AND ITS DETERMINANTS

Introduction

We have discussed the role of corporate entrepreneurship in the growth of Flipkart (Chapter 3), and the role of entrepreneurial culture in supporting corporate entrepreneurship in Flipkart (Chapter 4). However, ultimately, it is the management and the employees who are the key determinants of entrepreneurship in a firm, irrespective of its size, be it a start-up or a corporate enterprise. Given the management decision to promote entrepreneurship in an organization, it is the individual entrepreneurial behaviour of employees which is one of the primary antecedents of corporate entrepreneurship (Mustafa, et al., 2018). It is the entrepreneurial behaviour of employees which would matter the most because ultimately any corporate entrepreneurial activity must be initiated and implemented by groups/teams of individuals (de Jong, et al., 2011).

Accordingly, to analyse the role of individual employee characteristics and behaviours, de Jong et al. (2011) developed a measure for employees' intrapreneurial behaviour in organizations with a focus on three dimensions: namely innovativeness, proactiveness and risk-taking. An individual's behaviour is influenced by personal factors such as age, gender, education, hierarchy and tenure of employment, among others (Bandura, 1999), and these factors are also considered possible determinants of corporate entrepreneurship by de Jong, et al. (2011). It is against this backdrop that we decided to examine the determinants of corporate entrepreneurship in Flipkart, considering the characteristics and behaviour of managerial executives, given the support of top management.

At the outset, it is important to understand how employees perceive the style of management and the level of corporate entrepreneurship prevalent in Flipkart today, given their background characteristics, and how do perceived management style and employee background characteristics influence the level of corporate entrepreneurship currently prevalent in Flipkart.

To do this analysis, we developed a questionnaire comprising three sections. Section 1 focussed on education, age, gender, level of hierarchy in Flipkart, work experience in Flipkart and previous industry work/start-up founding experience of the chosen Flipsters, their self-assessment to know whether they are risk-takers, motivated to innovate, entrepreneurial and proactive. Educational qualifications are divided into graduation, post-graduation and doctorate degrees. No distinction is made between MBA and MSc or MTech degrees. For age, they are measured in terms of number of years completed as of 2022. Gender is identified in terms of male and female.

The levels of management hierarchy are divided into three groups: senior management (vice president and senior vice president), middle management (associate director, director and senior director), and junior management (junior manager, manager and senior manager). Work experience in Flipkart is measured in number of years and months, as is previous industry work/start-up founding experience. No distinction is made between industry work experience and start-up founding/work experience. Whether they are proactive, risk-takers, entrepreneurial, innovative and motivated is ascertained in terms of yes/no.

Section 2 ascertained their perception about the nature of management for pursuing corporate entrepreneurship in Flipkart currently, in terms of the four models of corporate entrepreneurship: The Enabler, The Producer, The Opportunist and The Advocate, proposed by Wolcott and Lippitz (2007). The respondents are asked to identify one of the four models. This is assumed to represent the current management style of Flipkart.

Section 3 comprised the Corporate Entrepreneurship Assessment Instrument (CEAI) developed by Kuratko, et al. (2014). Based on Section 3 of the questionnaire, we measured the level of corporate entrepreneurship prevailing in Flipkart today. Section 3 comprised 48 questions distributed under five sub-sections as follows:

(i) Management support for corporate entrepreneurship (19 questions)

(ii) Work discretion (10 questions)

(iii) Rewards/Reinforcement (6 questions)

(iv) Time availability (6 questions)

(v) Organizational boundaries (7 questions)

The respondents are asked to assign a score on a scale of 1 to 5. In general, the higher the score, the greater is the organization's support and implementation of corporate entrepreneurship strategy. The average score for each respondent (based on the responses for 48 questions) is calculated and identified as the level of internal environment for corporate entrepreneurship against each of the respondents. The overall average score indicates the level of corporate entrepreneurship prevalent in Flipkart, as perceived by management executives.

This questionnaire was sent by email to a select group of 76 managerial employees who were at different levels of hierarchy in different verticals in the organization. The questionnaire was sent by email at the beginning of February 2022, and 50 responses were received by the end of March 2022. Thus, it took about two months for us to obtain the completed questionnaire responses. Broadly, these 50 managerial employees are considered representative of the overall managerial workforce of the organization. Given this, at the outset it is essential to understand the key characteristics of these managerial employees.

Key Characteristics of Respondents

The education and knowledge base of Flipkart managerial employees as represented by the 50 respondents seemed impressive. The educational qualifications of respondents varied from BE/BTech to MBA/MS/MTech to PhD. A considerable majority (45) of the 50 respondents hold post-graduate degrees, mostly MBAs. Only two respondents are graduates and three respondents are PhDs.

The distribution of respondents in terms of age groups is presented in Table 5.1. Age is counted in terms of completed years as of 2022. In terms of age, more than one-half of the total is less than 40 years old, almost 2/5th of the total is between 40 and 49 years, whereas only the remaining respondents (8%) are more than 49 years old.

Table 5.1
Age of Respondents

Sl No.	Age groups	Number of Respondents	Percentage
1	30 to 39	27	54.00
2	40 to 49	19	38.00
3	50 to 59	4	8.00
4	Total	50	100.00

Table 5.2 presents the distribution of respondents in terms of previous industry work/start-up experience. More than one-half (54%) of the respondents do not have any previous work experience as they joined Flipkart as freshers after graduating from their respective institutions. One-fifth of

the respondents have a previous industry work/start-up experience of one to two years. About 14% respondents have previous industry work/start-up experience of more than two years and up to ten years, whereas 10% respondents have previous experience ranging from more than 10 years up to 25 years. Overall, it is Flipsters without any previous experience and candidates with work experience of one to two years who account for almost 74% of the total respondents.

Table 5.2
Previous Industry Work/Start-up Experience

Sl No.	Experience (in years)	Number of Respondents	Percentage
1	None	27	54.00
2	1 to 2	10	20.00
3	>2 to 5	4	8.00
4	>5 to 10	3	6.00
5	>10 to 25	5	10.00
6	>25 to 50	1	2.00
7	Total	50	100.00

The distribution of respondents in terms of work experience in Flipkart is given in Table 5.3. Since we have chosen only respondents with a minimum of three years of work experience in Flipkart, we do not have any respondents with less work experience. The threshold of three years is fixed to ensure that each respondent is able to adequately understand the work environment in the organization to respond to the questionnaire. A majority (82%) of the respondents have worked at Flipkart for a minimum of five years and a maximum of nine years. As many as 16% of the respondents have work experience of more than nine years, going up to 13 years.

In terms of gender, a majority of the workforce (70%) is male, the remaining (30%) being female. The levels of management hierarchy of respondents are presented in Table 5.4. The distribution indicates that middle management (comprising associate directors, directors, and senior directors) accounts for almost two-thirds (66%) of the total, whereas senior management (consisting of senior vice presidents and vice-presidents) accounts for one-fifth (20%) of the total. The remainder belong to junior management (including junior managers/managers/senior managers).

Table 5.3
Work Experience in Flipkart

Sl No.	Experience (in years)	Number of Respondents	Percentage
1	>3 to 5	1	2.00
2	>5 to 7	19	38.00
3	>7 to 9	22	44.00
4	>9 to 11	5	10.00
5	>11 to 13	3	6.00
6	Total	50	100.00

Table 5.4
Hierarchy of Management Employees

Sl No.	Hierarchy	Number of Respondents	Percentage
1	Senior management	10	20.00
2	Middle management	33	66.00
3	Junior management	7	14.00
4	Total	50	100.00

The five characteristics identified by the respondents are in terms of being risk-taking, innovative, entrepreneurial, motivated and proactive. Employees with such qualities are likely to contribute to corporate entrepreneurship in any organization, to varying degrees. That is why the questionnaire includes these questions along with those on management style and CEAI. Among the respondents, 82% identify themselves as risk takers, 92% as innovative, 90% as motivated, 72% as entrepreneurial, and 94% as proactive. This reveals that though a majority of the respondents claim to possess all five qualities, more than three-fourths of them agree to having entrepreneurial ambitions. This implies that the rest of the population (one-fourth) may be risk takers, innovative, proactive, and remain motivated but need not have entrepreneurial ambitions. This sums up the characteristics of respondents.

Management Style for Corporate Entrepreneurship

Management style is identified under four broad groups (Wolcott and Lippitz, 2007), as discussed in Chapter 2: the

Enabler, the Producer, the Opportunist, and the Advocate. The distribution as identified by the respondents is given in Table 5.5. A majority of the respondents (42%) have identified the Flipkart management style as Enabler, followed by Opportunist (26%), Advocate (22%), and Producer (nearly 10%). Broadly, this indicates that the Flipkart management is pro-corporate entrepreneurship, in the form of an Enabler, a Producer or an Advocate. Only about a quarter think that the management is opportunistic.

Table 5.5
Style of Management for Corporate Entrepreneurship

Sl No.	Experience (in years)	Number of Respondents	Percentage
1	The Enabler	21	42.00
2	The Producer	5	10.00
3	The Opportunist	13	26.00
4	The Advocate	11	22.00
5	Total	50	100.00

Level of Corporate Entrepreneurship and Its Determinants

The level of corporate entrepreneurship prevailing in Flipkart is identified under five sub-heads: namely, management support for entrepreneurship, work discretion, rewards and reinforcement, time availability, and organizational boundaries. Each respondent has ranked their responses to the questions on a scale from 1 to 5. The levels identified under each of the five sub-groups are given in Annexures (1 to 5). The distribution of respondents in terms of the levels of overall corporate entrepreneurship identified is presented in Table 5.6.

More than one-fourth of the respondents have identified the level of corporate entrepreneurship between 2 and 3, about two-thirds between 3 and 4, whereas only 6% identified it to be above 4 but less than 5, but none identified it below 2. The overall average stands at 3.30 for the 50 respondents. This implies that according to the respondents, the prevailing internal environment for corporate entrepreneurship in Flipkart is pretty conducive and above average, but there is immense scope for further improvement.

Table 5.6
Levels of Corporate Entrepreneurship as Identified by Respondents

Sl No.	Corporate Entrepreneurship Levels	Number of Respondents	Percentage
1	1 to 2	0	0
2	>2 to 3	14	28.00
3	>3 to 4	33	66.00
4	>4 to 5	3	6.00
5	Total	50	100.00

Given the level of corporate entrepreneurship, we ascertained from the respondents the impact it would have made on the corporate performance of the company. The respondents identified the impact on a Likert scale of 1 (least) to 5 (most), and the classified responses are given in Table 5.7. Among the respondents, 4% felt that corporate entrepreneurship had the least impact on corporate performance, 8% respondents felt it had less impact, 30% felt had a moderate impact, whereas 52% felt it had more impact and 6% felt it had the most impact on corporate performance. The overall average stands at 3.48 for the 50 respondents, implying that according to these Flipsters, corporate entrepreneurship has positively impacted Flipkart's corporate performance.

Table 5.7
Impact of Corporate Entrepreneurship on Corporate Performance

Sl No.	Impact levels	Number of Respondents	Percentage
1	Least	2	4.00
2	Less	4	8.00
3	Moderate	15	30.00
4	More	26	52.00
5	Most	3	6.00
6	Total	50	100.00

Given the above, the distribution of key variables with mean, standard deviation, minimum and maximum is presented in Table 5.8. ED, PE, PA, RT, IN, MO, ENT, GE, MS1, MS2, MS3 and MS4 are dummy variables and therefore vary between 0 and 1. ED is the dummy variable to distinguish postgraduates and PhDs (1) from graduates (0). PE is the dummy variable to distinguish those with previous work experience (1) from those without (0). PA is the dummy variable to distinguish those who are proactive (1) from those who are not (0). RT is the dummy variable to distinguish those who are risk-taking (1) from those who are not (0). IN is the dummy variable to distinguish those who are innovative (1) from those who are not (0). MO is the dummy variable to distinguish those who are motivated (1) from those who are not (0). ENT is the dummy variable to identify those who are entrepreneurial (1) from those who are not (0). GE is the gender dummy variable to separate males (1) from females (0). MS1 is the dummy variable to distinguish The Enabler (1) from the rest (0). MS2 is the dummy variable to separate the Advocate (1) from the rest. MS3 is the dummy variable to identify the Opportunist (1) from the rest (0). MS4 is the dummy variable to classify the Producer (1) from the rest (0).

AG represents the age of the respondents, varying from 30 to 56 years, the average being about 41 years. EX represents the experience of each respondent in Flipkart, in terms of number of years. EX varies from a minimum of 3.5 years to a maximum of almost 12 years, the average being less than 8 years. PE represents previous (industry work/start-up) experience of each respondent in terms of years. PE varies from nil to a maximum of 31 years, the average being less than 3.5 years. GR represents the grade or hierarchy of respondents ranging from 10 to 17, as identified by Flipkart HR group. CoE represents the overall level of corporate entrepreneurship as identified by the respondents. CoE varies from a minimum of 2.1 to a maximum of 4.43, the average being 3.30, implying a moderately high corporate entrepreneurship prevailing in Flipkart.

The correlation coefficients between the variables are presented in Table 5.9. All the values more than (+/-) 0.28 are statistically significant at 0.05 level. The variable that is of interest for our analysis is CoE. CoE has a statistically significant positive correlation (+0.35) only with PA, whereas it has a statistically significant negative correlation (-0.35) with MS3. AG has a statistically significant positive relationship with PE (+0.44), ENT (+0.38) and GR (+0.58). EX has a statistically negative positive relationship with PE (-0.28).

PE has a statistically significant positive relationship with MS4 (+0.29). PA has a positive relationship (+0.32) with RT. RT has a positive relationship with ENT (+0.40). MO has a positive relationship with IN (+0.39) and MS1 (+0.28). IN has a positive relationship with ENT (+0.47), GE (+0.45), and GR (+0.34). ENT has a positive relationship with GE (+0.36) and GR (+0.48). GE has a positive relationship with GR (+0.43). GR has a negative relationship with MS4 (-0.28). MS1 has a negative relationship with MS2 (+0.45), MS3 (-0.50) and MS4 (-0.28). MS2 has a negative relationship with MS3 (-0.31). All the other coefficients are statistically not significant.

Table 5.8
Summary Statistics

Variable	Observations	Mean	Std Deviation	Minimum	Maximum
AG	50	**41.12**	**5.88**	**30**	**56**
ED		.94	.24	0	1
EX		7.65	1.57	3.5	11.9
PE		3.37	6.65	0	31
PA		.94	.24	0	1
RT		.82	.39	0	1
IN		.92	.27	0	1
MO		.90	.30	0	1
ENT		.72	.45	0	1
GE		.70	.46	0	1
GR		14.24	1.70	10	17
MS1		.42	.50	0	1
MS2		.22	.42	0	1
MS3		.26	.44	0	1
MS4		.1	.30	0	1
CoE		3.30	.49	2.1	4.44

Given the above, we are keen to explore the key determinants of corporate entrepreneurship in Flipkart. We have taken CoE score as the dependent variable, whereas AD, ED, EX, PE, PA, IN, RT, MO, ENT, GE, GR, MS1, MS2, MS3 and MS4 are the explanatory variables. Thus, we hypothesise that management style and characteristics of managerial employees will have a significant influence on the level of corporate entrepreneurship prevailing in Flipkart. We carried out a stepwise (backward elimination) multiple regression analysis, with the following alternative equations:

CoE = f[AD, ED, EX, PE, PA, IN, RT, MO, ENT, GE, GR, MS1] __________ (1)

CoE = f[AD, ED, EX, PE, PA, IN, RT, MO, ENT, GE, GR, MS2] __________ (2)

CoE = f[AD, ED, EX, PE, PA, IN, RT, MO, ENT, GE, GR, MS3] __________ (3)

CoE = f[AD, ED, EX, PE, PA, IN, RT, MO, ENT, GE, GR, MS4] __________ (4)

Table 5.9
Correlation between the Variables

	CoE	AG	ED	EX	PE	PA	RT	MO	IN	ENT	GE	GR	MS1	MS2	MS3
CoE	1.00														
AG	-0.17	1.00													
ED	0.15	-0.20	1.00												
EX	0.18	-0.18	0.00	1.00											
PE	0.04	0.45	0.10	-0.29	1.00										
PA	0.35	0.09	-0.06	0.16	0.13	1.00									
RT	0.23	0.21	-0.11	0.19	0.15	0.32	1.00								
MO	0.24	0.06	-0.08	-0.12	0.09	-.08	0.02	1.00							
IN	0.08	0.20	-0.07	-0.18	0.11	-0.07	0.05	0.39	1.00						
ENT	-0.20	0.38	0.03	0.02	0.15	0.03	0.40	0.24	0.47	1.00					
GE	-0.07	0.16	0.20	-0.16	0.12	-0.17	0.03	0.07	0.45	0.37	1.00				
GR	-0.03	0.58	0.09	0.02	0.15	0.14	0.22	-0.11	0.35	0.49	0.43	1.00			
MS1	0.25	-0.12	0.22	0.01	-0.21	-0.13	-0.02	0.28	0.10	-0.10	0.20	-0.07	1.00		
MS2	0.11	-0.14	0.13	0.08	-0.18	0.13	0.12	-0.14	-0.02	0.01	-0.18	0.04	-0.45	1.00	
MS3	-0.36	0.26	-0.23	-0.02	0.20	-0.04	-0.20	-0.26	-0.16	0.07	-0.01	0.24	-0.50	-0.31	1.00
MS4	-0.03	0.01	-0.20	-0.09	0.30	0.08	0.16	0.11	0.10	0.06	-0.07	-0.29	-0.28	-0.18	-0.20

The four (stepwise multiple regression) models described above will ascertain how the four different management styles differ in terms of their impact on CoE, in addition to other explanatory variables. In this regard, a description of stepwise (backward elimination) multiple regression is in order. Stepwise (backward elimination) multiple regression, at the outset, will consider all the explanatory variables included in a model, but it will eliminate those variables which do not have a statistically significant contribution to the dependent variable, stepwise. Finally, it will lead to the selection of those explanatory variables which have statistically significant coefficients and therefore can be considered 'best predictors' of the dependent variable. Thus, stepwise regression involves developing a sequence of linear models leading to the identification of the fewest predictors of dependent variables (Lewis, 2007). Though stepwise modelling has several disadvantages (Whittingham, et al., 2006), it is useful, particularly in exploratory research as a screening tool. The present study is exploratory in nature and, therefore, we feel it is appropriate for the proposed analysis. The summary results of the four stepwise (backward elimination) regression models are presented in Table 5.10. The analysis is done by using Stata 11 software and we reported the regression coefficients with t values, F values and adjusted R^2 values. It is important to note that all the four models retained MO, PA, IN, ED, RT and ENT (at 0.10 statistical significance), and eliminated GE, PE, GR, EX, AD, and MS1, Ms2, M3, and M4 respectively. All the four models are statistically significant at 0.00 level as indicated by their respective F values. The adjusted R^2 values indicate that the models have an explanatory power of more than 37%. The F values, adjusted R^2 values, and t values of all the statistically significant variables are identical (though the sequence of retention of statistically significant variables and the sequence of elimination of statistically insignificant variables vary from one model to another).

The eliminated variables indicate that gender (GE), age (AD), hierarchy (GR), previous industry work/start-up experience (PE), and tenure of work experience in Flipkart (EX), and the four alternative management styles (MS1, MS2, MS3 and MS4) in four different models do not have any influence on CoE. The management style does not make any difference to the significance/insignificance of the remaining explanatory variables between the four models. There is no multicollinearity problem as the VIF values range between 1.04 and 1.63 for the five statistically significant variables (mean VIF value being 1.32), much less than the threshold value of 4 (Hair, et al., 2010).

Table 5.10
Determinants of Corporate Entrepreneurship—Stepwise (backward elimination) Multiple Regression Analysis Results

Variables	Model 1	Model 2	Model 3	Model 4
MO	.5220467 (2.61)**	.5220467 (2.61)**	.5220467 (2.61)**	.5220467 (2.61)**
PA	.641551 (2.61)**	.641551 (2.61)**	.641551 (2.61)**	.641551 (2.61)**
IN	.4253116 (1.72)*	.4253116 (1.72)*	.4253116 (1.72)*	.4253116 (1.72)*

ED	.5660845 (2.40)**	.5660845 (2.40)**	.5660845 (2.40)**	.5660845 (2.40)**
RT	.4701336 (2.78)**	.4701336 (2.78)**	.4701336 (2.78)**	.4701336 (2.78)**
ENT	-.6014675 (-3.86)***	-.6014675 (-3.86)***	-.6014675 (-3.86)***	-.6014675 (-3.86)***
Constant	1.355824 (3.20)***	1.355824 (3.20)***	1.355824 (3.20)***	1.355824 (3.20)***
F value	5.84	5.84	5.84	5.84
Adj. R2	0.3720	0.3720	0.3720	0.3720
No. of observations	50	50	50	50
	Sequence of Eliminated Variables			
	GR	GR	PE	GR
	PE	PE	GR	MS4
	GE	MS2	GE	PE
	MS1	GE	MS3	GE
	AG	AG	AG	AG
	EX	EX	EX	EX
Variable		VIF	1/VIF	
ENT		1.63	0.614020	
IN		1.49	0.669995	
RT		1.41	0.710539	
MO		1.20	0.833759	
PA		1.14	0.880349	
ED		1.04	0.956988	
Mean VIF		1.32		
Note: All the F values are significant at 0.0001 level				

****Significant at 0.000 level; **Significant at 0.05 level; *Significant at 0.10 level*

The six statistically significant variables are MO, PA, IN, ED, RT and ENT. Of these, ED is the dummy variable to distinguish post-graduates and PhDs (1) from graduates (0). This implies that the contribution of doctorates and postgraduates to CoE is positive and statistically significant, and distinctly different from that of graduates. Further, it is the motivated (MO), innovative (IN), proactive (PA) and risk-taking (RT) managerial executives who contribute positively to CoE significantly, whereas those who are entrepreneurial (ENT) do otherwise. This has important implications in the context of the organization.

Corporate entrepreneurship in an organization is predominantly determined by the management and its key techno-managerial employees (as discussed in the previous two chapters). Given this, we are keen to ascertain what the key determining variables of corporate entrepreneurship in Flipkart are. Accordingly, we conducted a survey among key managerial executives to probe: whether Flipkart management is supportive to corporate entrepreneurship, and if yes, in what form? Given their age, gender, hierarchy in the organization, previous industry work/start-up experience, education, and duration of work experience in Flipkart, how do their qualities (in terms of proactiveness, innovativeness, motivation, risk-taking and entrepreneurial behaviour) influence the level of corporate entrepreneurship prevailing in Flipkart?

This is because, ultimately, any corporate entrepreneurial activity is initiated and implemented by (a group of) individuals (de Jong, et al., 2011). The strength of an organization lies in its employees, more than anything else. Among others, corporate entrepreneurship is influenced by motivation, individual skills and perceived environmental dynamism of employees (Fini, et al., 2012). Miller (1983) views an entrepreneurial organization to comprise individuals who are innovative and proactive and have risk-taking behaviours. It is the individuals' intrapreneurial behaviour, defined as the identification and exploitation of opportunities by individual workers to advance the organization, and reflected in their innovative, proactive and risk-taking behaviors, which would profoundly influence the pursuance of corporate entrepreneurship (de Jong, et al., 2011). Accordingly, we have ascertained the key qualities of select (50) managerial executives with respect to proactiveness, innovativeness, risk-taking, motivation and entrepreneurship.

Given the level of corporate entrepreneurship in Flipkart and the scope for improving it further, managerial executives have to be proactive, innovative, motivated, and risk-takers, with postgraduate and doctorate qualifications, if Flipkart has to achieve a higher level of corporate entrepreneurship in the future.

The start-up ideas of many were germinated in Flipkart, thanks to brainstorming with colleagues, mentoring received from colleagues and other experts in the organization, interactions with ex-Flipsters who are start-up founders now, and cultivating networks with angels and VCs, among others. They also understand that with Flipkart on their resume, it would be relatively easy to obtain funds, markets, human resources and mentors, once they move out of their jobs to set up their start-ups. They are also aware of the fact that many ex-Flipsters have emerged successful as start-up founders and investors-cum-mentors, after exiting from the company. This has, of course, enabled Flipkart to contribute substantially to the start-up ecosystem in various forms, as discussed in the previous chapter. But this could come at a cost. Managerial executives with entrepreneurial ambitions will work on promoting their own ideas in addition to contributing to promoting corporate entrepreneurship within the organization.

On the other hand, if the company prefers to have more and more managerial executives who are talented in terms of higher education qualifications (postgraduation and PhD), innovativeness, proactiveness, risk-taking, and motivation, the company will gain from such employees. Higher levels of education, particularly technical education, make powerful contributions to technology creation and diffusion (UNDP, 2001). Higher levels of technical education would represent higher talent and higher capability, among others, and therefore, such managerial employees will be able to identify and exploit opportunities due to better prior knowledge and better capacities to acquire external resources and to accumulate new knowledge and skills (Unger, et al., 2011). Higher educated people with higher human capital are more likely to be proactive and innovative and take risks (de Jong, et al., 2011). Therefore, they are able to contribute significantly to corporate entrepreneurship.

Proactiveness of employees would bring multiple benefits to an organization. It is an opportunity-seeking, forward-looking perspective of employees with high awareness of external developments which prompt them to act in anticipation (Rauch, et. al., 2009). Proactiveness is associated with taking initiatives to pursue new opportunities (Lumpkin and Dess, 1996) and taking the lead rather than following in key business areas (Covid and Slevin, 1989). Parker et al. (2006, p. 295) define proactive behavior as 'self-initiated and future-oriented action that aims to change and improve the situation or oneself.' The proactive behaviour of employees brings multiple benefits to an organization. It improves the internal organizational environment such as improving work methods or influencing work of colleagues (Parker and Collins, 2010). Such employees put in constructive efforts voluntarily to bring out organization-wide functional change with respect to how work is executed, make innovative suggestions or recommendations for change, and individually implement ideas. All these would contribute distinctly to corporate entrepreneurship.

Innovative employees are always a boon to any company. They would take initiatives in establishing a new spin-off organization, or identifying a new market opportunity and capitalizing on it, or achieving product and/or process innovations, or improving business routines, or even bringing new employees with similar characteristics (Amo, 2010). It would involve any opportunity utilized or action taken by such employees for deviating from the status quo, to strengthen and promote their organization (Jong, et al., 2010). Such employees will be able to perceive challenges and opportunities more appropriately at the right time for the benefit of the organization. Such actions invariably contribute to promoting corporate entrepreneurship strategy in an organization.

Risk-taking behaviour involves taking bold actions by

venturing into the unknown and committing resources heavily to new initiatives in unknown environments (Rauch, et al., 2009). Corporate entrepreneurship activities such as innovation, reorganization, business vertical diversification and M&As involve considerable risk, as these call for investment of time, effort and resources, much before rewards emerge from such actions. In fact, many of the senior management executives of Flipkart have admitted that they believe in calculated risk-taking. Challenging the status quo constantly is an important characteristic of such risk-taking employees (Antoncic and Hisrich, 2003). Calculated risk takers bring gains for the organization.

Motivation is defined as an individual's willingness to act (Rothschild, 1999; Siemsen, et al., 2008). Motivation which involves knowledge generation as well as knowledge sharing within an organization is imperative to pursue corporate entrepreneurship (Stevenson and Jarillo, 1990). When employees within an organization are motivated to generate and exchange information between colleagues, it creates value for both, leading to greater innovation.

Higher education, proactiveness, risk-taking and motivation are important drivers for people to exhibit their entrepreneurial nature and contribute to corporate entrepreneurship in Flipkart. These key drivers further enable people to pursue their entrepreneurial journey while working for the organization, while brainstorming, being mentored, developing networks, exploring funds, searching for the right partners, etc. In fact, in its history of more than a decade, Flipkart has periodically experienced the exit of highly talented employees for the subsequent creation of start-ups. As of now, more than 200 start-ups have emerged from ex-Flipsters, of which hardly one quarter have failed and exited from the market. Thus, with the ratio of success to failure being 3:1, many Flipsters are motivated to think of entrepreneurship outside of Flipkart. Such entrepreneurs have contributed to the enhanced visibility and reputation of Flipkart and also underlined its contribution to the start-up ecosystem of the country in general, and that of Bangalore in particular.

Summary

We have ascertained the key determinants of corporate entrepreneurship in Flipkart by taking into consideration the perceived style of management, on the one hand, and characteristics and behaviour of 50 managerial employees of Flipkart, on the other. The style of management for corporate entrepreneurship did not matter. The age, gender, hierarchy, previous industry work/start-up experience and tenure of work experience in Flipkart did not matter either. What mattered were higher educational qualifications, proactiveness, innovativeness, motivation, and risk-taking behaviour of these managerial executives, positively contributing to corporate entrepreneurship. Entrepreneurship-minded executives may emerge as start-up founders in the future, thereby contributing to the start-up ecosystem and entrepreneurial culture.

Thus, the important inference and implication of this analysis for Flipkart is that it is advisable to recruit managerial employees who have postgraduate or doctorate qualifications, and are proactive, innovative, motivated and risk-taking. At the same time, recruiting those who have an entrepreneurial bent of mind might benefit Flipkart in the form of emergence of entrepreneurial ventures from ex-Flipsters (i.e., after such executives exit from the organization) and account for its ecosystem contributions in terms of start-ups and nurturing an entrepreneurial culture.

Annexures

Annexure 5.1
Management Support for Entrepreneurship

Sl No.	Management Support Levels	Number of Respondents	Percentage
1	1 to 2	4	8.00
2	2 to 3	15	30.77
3	3 to 4	25	50.00
4	4 to 5	6	12.00
5	Total	50	100.00

Annexure 5.2
Work Discretion

Sl No.	Work Discretion Levels	Number of Respondents	Percentage
1	1 to 2	0	0
2	2 to 3	12	24.00
3	3 to 4	28	56.00
4	4 to 5	10	20.00
5	Total	50	100.00

Annexure 5.3
Rewards/Reinforcement

Sl No.	Rewards/ Reinforcement Levels	Number of Respondents	Percentage
1	1 to 2	1	2.00
2	2 to 3	5	10.00
3	3 to 4	30	60.00
4	4 to 5	14	28.00
5	Total	50	100.00

Annexure 5.4
Time Availability

Sl No.	Time Availability	Number of Respondents	Percentage
1	1 to 2	1	2.00
2	2 to 3	33	66.00
3	3 to 4	16	32.00
4	4 to 5	0	0
5	Total	50	100.00

Annexure 5.5
Organizational Boundaries

Sl No.	Organizational Boundaries	Number of Respondents	Percentage
1	1 to 2	1	2.00
2	2 to 3	12	24.00
3	3 to 4	33	66.00
4	4 to 5	4	8.00
5	Total	50	100.00

6

SUMMARY AND CONCLUSIONS

Context of the Study

The emergence, stability and growth of firms have challenges as well as implications for policymakers and empirical researchers. Among all, in the last couple of decades, tech start-ups along with their ecosystems have been emerging rapidly across the world, particularly in the developed and emerging economies. However, a substantial proportion of these tech start-ups fail and exit from the markets in the initial years after their emergence. A minor proportion of them survive and a fraction of the survived ones scale up, register accelerated growth, and thereby make a significant impact on the economy. This holds good for Indian tech start-ups and their ecosystems as well.

Though Indian tech start-ups and their ecosystems are of relatively recent origin, they have been gaining global traction due to their rapid growth since the early 2010s.

Today India has the third-largest start-up ecosystem in the world. Bangalore has had consistent global recognition as the best start-up ecosystem in India. Considered the 'start-up capital of India', Bangalore has accounted for a major share of tech start-ups as well as unicorns in India every year, consistently for almost a decade now. Flipkart stands apart as it is one of the earliest Indian unicorns that emerged in Bangalore and has grown to become one of the largest e-commerce companies in India since its birth in 2007.

Given its growth trajectory, Flipkart can be considered a high-growth company as it has registered an astounding growth performance in terms of both revenue and employment since its inception. What is more commendable is that Flipkart's growth contribution is not just confined to financial or economic ratios but extends beyond, in terms of varied contributions (such as a market for other start-ups through M&As, a source of finance, human resources, mentors, incubators and entrepreneurship, among others) to the start-up ecosystem of India in general, and that of Bangalore in particular. This is in addition to the support system it has created for marketing India's informal and disadvantaged sectors. Thus, Flipkart has defined a distinctly unique growth path—in the process of its own growth since inception—for future tech start-ups in India.

Flipkart founders Binny Bansal and Sachin Bansal gained experience at two different tech start-ups. Their time at these companies, combined with their education at IIT Delhi, helped them recognize an entrepreneurial opportunity. This is a clear case of 'knowledge spillover', where their prior experiences and skills contributed to their success in creating Flipkart, an outcome of their ideation and its commercialization.

However, the two co-founders had no clear idea about the future performance of the start-up when they created it. It was through a process of continuous learning and undivided 'customer obsession' that the Flipkart founders realized their superior managerial efficiency, which led to its accelerated growth in the start-up phase and beyond. The superior managerial efficiency acquired (through customer obsession) subsequently led them to pursue a strategy of corporate entrepreneurship as a means to achieve sustained competitiveness for long-term growth.

Thus, 'knowledge spillover' and 'superior efficiency' as realized by the founders of Flipkart would have played a decisive role in its emergence as a start-up and growth during and beyond its start-up phase. But it is the long-term growth of Flipkart and its current contributions that deserve a critical examination. Our preliminary enquiries and exploration led us to conclude that the pursuance of 'corporate entrepreneurship' has played a significant role in the long-term phenomenal growth of Flipkart. It is against this backdrop that a detailed literature review was carried out.

Corporate Entrepreneurship Domain: Significance and Key Research Gaps

Entrepreneurship is generally associated with start-ups. Entrepreneurs are, by definition, creators of ideas, jobs and economic value. They create value where none existed earlier. Such entrepreneurs take calculated risks with persistence and resoluteness to achieve their dreams with big rewards. As their new venture succeeds and grows, a structured organization emerges. However, with growth, a firm develops inertia, staleness, complex processes, and rigid bureaucracy with hierarchy. When a start-up venture becomes a corporate venture, it poses new challenges for its subsequent growth. That is, sustaining or accelerating growth is a greater challenge for large established firms relative to smaller firms.

As a corporate venture acquires a bureaucratic structure with rules and regulations for its employees to follow, the organization tends to lose its dynamism and become rigid and inflexible. In the process, the organization develops resistance to change and loses its innovative and entrepreneurial spirit. Thus, preserving the entrepreneurial spirit becomes a challenge as an organization grows in size and age. As a result, its ability to grow further would eventually diminish. To overcome the challenges for growth, a firm has to achieve sustainable competitive advantage. Towards this end, nurturing the entrepreneurial spirit and an innovative environment becomes imperative. Corporate entrepreneurship has emerged (since the early 1970s) as a strategy to overcome organizational inertia, inflexibility and lack of innovation in large public firms. It is considered a potential viable means of enhancing and sustaining corporate competitiveness to achieve high levels of organizational performance.

Corporate entrepreneurship within established organizations comprises creation of new businesses (through intrapreneurs), strategic renewal, and innovation. Thus, corporate entrepreneurship has three important dimensions: innovation, corporate venturing, and strategic renewal. Though empirical researchers have defined the scope and domain of corporate entrepreneurship in different ways, there has been a greater convergence since the mid-1990s on what constitutes corporate entrepreneurship. Broadly, it comprises innovation, venturing or intrapreneuring, and strategic renewal (for organizational transformation) within existing firms.

Corporate entrepreneurship strategy is pursued to sustain business dynamism, vitality, innovativeness and entrepreneurship, to achieve competitive advantages for long-term growth. In the process, it steadily achieves greater customer value and market share for accelerated growth. It is a means of achieving business development and growth in revenue and profits. Thus, the ultimate objective of pursuing corporate entrepreneurship by a large organization is to achieve higher levels of corporate performance, growth and profitability.

Given this, corporate entrepreneurship in general is implemented in multiple ways including new venture creation, setting up new autonomous units within and/or outside the company, mergers and acquisitions, innovation, proactively reorganizing the structure of the company, partnering with other companies, etc. It is a process that involves accumulating, converting and leveraging resources for gaining a competitive edge in the form of developing product, process and organizational innovations to rejuvenate and redefine or transform the firm and its markets and industries. Exploiting entrepreneurial opportunities and transforming business organizations through innovations are the key dimensions of corporate entrepreneurship strategy, which have been mostly pursued by large growing companies, though firms of different sizes would find it advantageous to pursue in the process of growth.

This calls for nurturing an entrepreneurial spirit and innovative climate at all organizational levels, from the top management down the hierarchy to each individual employee at the operational levels. Given this, there is no uniform strategy for corporate entrepreneurship which can be applied across firms of different sizes in different regions. Each firm may adopt its own innovative corporate entrepreneurship strategy. It would depend on a firm's management style, management goals stated in its vision and mission, the way its employees are given freedom and encouragement, availability of resources, the quality of human resources acquired and nurtured, etc.

However, pursuing corporate entrepreneurship strategy is not an easy task, nor would it occur spontaneously. It would call for consistent efforts to build internal capabilities and acquire capabilities and knowledge from outside through mergers and acquisitions, and partnerships, among others. Corporate entrepreneurship strategy does not always ensure success, as it is a rough-and-tumble process with few guarantees. Some attempts may succeed and others may fail. Thus, it is essentially a learning process.

Given this, much of the literature on corporate entrepreneurship is confined to conceptual and theoretical issues, with very few empirical data-based analyses. The empirical exploration of corporate entrepreneurship has predominantly revolved around large established firms in the context of the developed world, with hardly any studies emanating from SMEs in emerging economies like India. Existing literature has rarely revealed how a firm that pursued corporate entrepreneurship strategy over time has contributed to the ecosystem. Further, it is not yet clear how corporate entrepreneurship strategy emerges and aids organizational growth over time, particularly in a company that emerged as a start-up and continues to grow in an accelerated manner to become a leading company in the sector. The need to nurture entrepreneurial culture as part of a corporate entrepreneurship strategy in an organization has not been adequately described, nor have the determinants of corporate entrepreneurship in a growing organization emerged clearly from existing literature. The research objectives, scope and methods of analysis are refined against this backdrop, with an exclusive focus on Flipkart.

Objectives, Scope and Methods of Research Exploration

We have explored three research objectives with respect to Flipkart (since its inception in October 2007 till April 2022), covering a spectrum of about 15 years. At first, we traced the origin, growth and ecosystem contributions of Flipkart and its determinants, in the context of corporate entrepreneurship. Subsequently, we proposed a corporate entrepreneurship model as it emerged in the context of Flipkart. Secondly, we examined the key characteristics of entrepreneurial culture, as part of its corporate entrepreneurship strategy, as prevalent in Flipkart today. Thirdly, we ascertained the current level of corporate entrepreneurship in Flipkart and analysed its determinants.

The first research objective was explored based on secondary data on Flipkart available in the public domain, including media reports. We developed a 'chronology of events' (from October 2007 till April 2022) describing the major developments that have contributed to the growth of the company. Based on these descriptions, we analysed the key contributors to the growth of the company over a period of time, in terms of building its supply capabilities (technology and products) to steadily increase its product offerings, diversifying its business verticals as a means of growth, and ensuring a steady increase in demand for its ever-expanding product portfolios. Subsequently, we examined the ecosystem contributions made by Flipkart to the start-up ecosystem in Bangalore and beyond. Finally, we derived inferences to develop 'a model of corporate entrepreneurship' that emerged from Flipkart.

The second research objective was analysed based on primary data obtained through personal interviews (through an interview protocol each) with five categories of respondents: namely, the current CEO Kalyan Krishnamurthy, co-founder/director Binny Bansal, tenured senior executives (including two intrapreneurs), founders of start-ups acquired by Flipkart, and founders of start-ups created by ex-Flipkart employees (known as ex-Flipsters). While the CEO and the co-founder represented ownership and management, tenured executives (including intrapreneurs) and founders of acquired start-ups who are currently Flipkart employees together represented top management involved in decision-making and/or implementation. Founders of start-ups created by ex-Flipsters and operating outside Flipkart represented former Flipkart employees. The primary data gathered through personal interviews from these different groups of stakeholders formed the basis for qualitative analysis of the second research objective. Thus, we adopted triangulation of three different data sources (data triangulation) to elicit the presence and characteristics of entrepreneurial culture in Flipkart.

To analyse the third research objective, we gathered primary data from a select group of 50 Flipkart executives by circulating a questionnaire over email. The objective of the questionnaire was to elicit information on the level of corporate entrepreneurship, and the factors which contributed to or determined the level of corporate entrepreneurship prevalent in Flipkart. For this purpose, the questionnaire comprised a Corporate Entrepreneurship Assessment Instrument (CEAI). Furthermore, we ascertained the nature of resource authority and organizational ownership prevailing in Flipkart, by means of four models of corporate entrepreneurship to represent management style. In addition, the background characteristics (age, work experience in Flipkart, previous work/industry experience, education, and gender) of the respondents—including whether they were proactive, motivated, risk-taker, innovative, and entrepreneurial—were obtained. The average scores for various questions in the CEAI helped determine the level of corporate entrepreneurship at Flipkart. Additionally, a backward elimination regression analysis, using corporate entrepreneurship level as the dependent variable and management style, background, and characteristics of respondents as explanatory variables, identified the key determinants of corporate entrepreneurship.

For gathering primary data from personal interviews and through the questionnaire, respondents were chosen with purpose or by personal judgement. This non-probability sampling technique was chosen to ensure a representative sample by using sound judgement. We ensured that the respondents had adequate information and were knowledgeable about Flipkart, and that they could enable our in-depth investigation and provide answers for the two research questions.

Corporate Entrepreneurship and Entrepreneurial Culture in Flipkart: Findings

The growth of Flipkart since its emergence as an online bookstore in October 2007 has been eventful, characterized by a steady diversification of product portfolios through business verticals, introduction of innovative business strategies in terms of supply chain and logistics, marketing and finance, and acquisition of multiple early-stage tech start-ups, apart from occasional partnerships with other firms. At the same time, Flipkart experienced the intermittent exit of talented and ambitious executives who later set up their own tech start-ups. Overall, Flipkart could achieve phenomenal growth in the nascent Indian e-commerce sector, to emerge as one of the largest e-commerce companies in the country. Flipkart's steady success is evident not only in its performance at the firm level, such as revenue and employment, but also in its significant contributions to the start-up ecosystem of Bangalore and beyond. These contributions include providing ideas, markets, finance, human resources, mentors, incubation support, and fostering an entrepreneurial culture. The driving force of these significant contributions has been its resolute and committed focus on the Indian consumer (its 'customer-first approach'), which has continued despite changes in management and ownership during 2007–2022.

In India's nascent e-commerce industry of the late 2000s, even in its best start-up ecosystem of Bangalore that was still evolving (Bala Subrahmanya, 2017), a start-up faced the dual challenges of creating supply capability and generating demand. For creating supply capability, Flipkart founders/management resorted to building capability internally and organically, supplemented by acquiring capability externally and inorganically through M&As of early-stage start-ups and partnerships with complementary start-ups, from its early days. M&As facilitated multiple objectives such as business diversification, acquisition of talent and market, and acquisition of patents, among others. A significant feature of the Flipkart growth story has been its unprecedented success with respect to M&As.

Simultaneously, the founders and management periodically raised finance. The initial growth performance and early attainment of the status of unicorn made further fundraising smooth. Steady talent acquisition and accumulation driven by 'ambitious and audacious management' enabled Flipkart to start new ventures/platforms within, though not all of them succeeded. Successful new ventures contributed to infrastructure development through process innovations. Thus, talent base, M&As and partnerships, innovative intrapreneurial ventures, and periodic fundraising led to a steady expansion as well as diversification of business verticals (with economies of scale as well as of scope). The latter led to an increase in Flipkart's product offerings from just one in 2007 to 80 by 2022. This is how Flipkart succeeded in creating its supply capability.

However, the founders and management had realized early on that in a nascent industry where customers were only used to offline shopping, 'supply will not create its own demand' and therefore generating demand was a bigger challenge. Demand dimensions had multiple complexities, such as the notoriety gained by the e-commerce industry due to fly-by-night operators who collected money from multiple customers but never delivered the products and ceased to exist thereafter. Customers enjoyed the comfort, convenience and trust associated with offline shopping. Furthermore, the internet infrastructure for online purchases was underdeveloped and inconsistent. Another challenge was fragmented consumers in terms of income groups, with lower-income consumers accounting for a vast majority. The realization of these 'harsh realities' of the Indian consumer market prompted the founders/management to resort to innovative financial and marketing strategies.

Flipkart introduced 'cash on delivery' for the first time in the Indian market, winning over customers and successfully overcoming the trust deficit in the online market. This was soon supplemented by a 30-day 'no questions asked' return policy, which significantly contributed to the further building of visibility and credibility. The innovative 'kids as adults' advertisement further boosted consumer demand. Certain

M&As expanded Flipkart's customer base along with aiding the diversification of business verticals. A targeted credit card, schemes such as 'buy now, pay later', 'no cost EMI', 'loan offer', and 'refurbished goods market' have played a decisive role in converting a significant proportion of 'consumer desires' of the lower-middle income group and lower-income group customers into 'consumer demand'. All this together led to a steady increase in consumer demand to go with a steady increase in supply, and culminated in Flipkart's unprecedented growth story. Thus, the simultaneous focus of the founders and management on supply creation and demand generation is the unique feature of the corporate entrepreneurship model that emerged out of Flipkart.

Along with its unprecedented growth, Flipkart has made noteworthy contributions to start-up ecosystems in Bangalore and beyond. It has played a key role in the emergence of innumerable start-up entrepreneurs, angels and venture capitalists for start-up funding, market for early-stage start-ups, human resource talent and mentors for start-up creation and operations, partnership support for upcoming start-ups, and incubation and acceleration support for start-up nurturing, among others.

Another vital contribution was creating a support system for micro, small and medium enterprises (MSMEs), which is the employment backbone of the Indian economy, particularly the informal sector and women enterprises. Flipkart promotes entrepreneurial culture and also drives media support for start-ups across the country. Thus, Flipkart has emerged as a major entrepreneurial ecosystem-supporting pillar in India

But all these would not have been possible without

promoting 'entrepreneurial culture' within the organization. A firm with an entrepreneurial culture audaciously and regularly innovates, is proactive, and assumes risks to carry out strategies to develop innovative products, services or processes. Entrepreneurial culture promotes new ideas, enables experimenting, and generates solutions to problems, ultimately contributing to organizational innovativeness. Such an organization will experience positive outcomes in the form of new technologies, products, services and processes, ultimately enhancing firm performance and resulting in sustainable competitive advantages.

To explore the presence and characteristics of entrepreneurial culture in Flipkart, we made use of primary data gathered from three broad groups of Flipkart stakeholders: CEO and co-founder/director, tenured executives including intrapreneurs and founders of acquired start-ups (through M&As), and founders of start-ups (founded subsequent to their exit from Flipkart, i.e., by ex-Flipsters). This facilitated data triangulation. The convergence of views between the three groups of stakeholders substantiated the presence of entrepreneurial culture in Flipkart and the corporate entrepreneurship model developed based on time-series (secondary) data.

The 'customer-first approach' and audacious goals made Flipkart management take quick decisions. Undivided customer focus enabled Flipkart to attract, engage and motivate 'top talent' to drive innovations. Entry barriers for prospective employees are high, and once recruited, employees and teams are given complete autonomy. Employees are encouraged to experiment and to challenge the status quo on a continuous basis, and provided resources for risk-taking. Employee empowerment is the hallmark of Flipkart. New ideas are encouraged not only from the top but also from the grassroots level. Bureaucracy is limited, and failure is tolerated, not penalized. Such an environment is conducive to innovations, and that is why Flipkart produced process/market/financial innovations periodically. Periodic introduction of innovations is another hallmark of Flipkart's growth. It facilitated periodic M&As and, in turn, diversification of business verticals, talent and patent acquisitions, and market expansion. M&As further induced innovations. Together, they contributed to a steady increase in supply as well as demand, leading to the phenomenal growth of Flipkart.

The presence of entrepreneurial culture and the pursuance of corporate entrepreneurship as a means of competitive advantage necessitated a quantitative exploration of the level of corporate entrepreneurship prevailing in Flipkart, and its determinants. Primary data gathered from 50 managerial executives of Flipkart revealed that the presence of corporate entrepreneurship in Flipkart was moderately high, indicating the scope for further improvement. Given this, it is important to understand what contributed to the level of corporate entrepreneurship in Flipkart.

Our primary data-based analysis revealed that neither the style of Flipkart management nor age, gender, hierarchy, previous industry work/start-up experience and tenure of work experience in Flipkart of managerial executives contributed to corporate entrepreneurship. It was the higher educational qualifications, proactiveness, innovativeness, motivation and risk-taking by managerial executives which made positive contributions, whereas those who were entrepreneurial in nature did not contribute to corporate entrepreneurship. This implies that it is advisable to recruit managerial executives who have postgraduate or doctorate qualifications, and are proactive, innovative, motivated and risk-taking by nature. The entrepreneurial culture and entrepreneurial bent of mind amongst employees helped them shape their independent journeys, contributing to the Flipkart ecosystem in terms of start-ups and entrepreneurial culture promotion.

Flipkart's Growth through Corporate Entrepreneurship Strategy and Promotion of Entrepreneurial Culture: Inferences and Implications

The founders and management of Flipkart pursued their start-up growth strategy judiciously in a yet-underdeveloped tech-intensive industry, in an emerging economy riddled with infrastructural constraints for supply and characterized by low-income consumer groups dominating demand. The 'single-minded focus on customers' or 'customer obsession' prompted the founders/management to take early steps to develop infrastructure to build supply capability, on the one hand, and gain customer confidence to divert customers accustomed to offline shopping towards online shopping, on the other hand.

While building infrastructure was found imperative, that alone was not adequate for a steady growth of supply. Further, focussing on a single product for 'scale expansion' with the available technology talent to achieve economies of scale was considered not sufficient to achieve robust growth. Therefore, product diversification through multiple business verticals (through organic and inorganic M&A routes) to achieve 'economies of scope' was brought in as a supplementary strategy. As part of the organic route, entrepreneurial culture was nurtured through motivated, risk-taking employees by providing them with resources for creating innovative new ventures within Flipkart. Audacious goals set by the management and corresponding bold experiments by the employees together contributed to successful innovations and successful M&As.

Thus, Flipkart has exhibited how a start-up can achieve a steady supply growth in an infant industry in an evolving start-up ecosystem in an emerging economy. Calculated risk-taking and bold experiments are inevitable for a start-up in an uncertain business environment. Similarly, a start-up need not wait to stabilize its growth through 'scale expansion mode' only. With in-house technology strength, it can explore 'scope expansion mode' simultaneously. For both, raising adequate finance and recruiting talented human resources periodically are imperative. Thus, Flipkart founders/management have simultaneously worked on production, marketing, finance and human resources, and achieved success. This is a case to learn from and emulate for prospective start-up founders in the Indian start-up ecosystem.

The demand-side management by Flipkart is equally innovative. Winning over the confidence of the growing number of 'offline customers' was the biggest challenge for the founders/management. This challenge was particularly formidable because there were hardly any established e-commerce companies with a good track record in India (when Flipkart was born), and the market was marred by many fly-by-night operators. By and large, customers were accustomed to visiting shops, seeing the products, physically checking quality and price, and then deciding to purchase. Such a facility was not just available in online shopping. To overcome these deficiencies and win over 'customer trust', Flipkart introduced the 'cash on delivery' scheme and a 30-day 'no questions asked' return policy, which significantly contributed to gaining customer confidence.

Equally innovative was how Flipkart converted 'consumer desire' to 'consumer demand' through a series of schemes such as 'buy now, pay later', no cost EMI, loan offers, promotion of refurbished goods market, introduction of an exclusive credit card, etc. Many other Indian e-commerce companies have subsequently followed these innovations, which reflect the impact it has made on consumer confidence and the successful conversion of desire into demand in the Indian market. This is another key lesson to learn and emulate for prospective start-up founders in the Indian start-up ecosystem.

It is the simultaneous focus on supply and demand through nurturing entrepreneurial culture and pursuing corporate entrepreneurship by means of innovation, new ventures, and periodical organizational restructuring which has overseen the transformation of Flipkart from a start-up to achieving the status of a 'high growth, high impact' company in India, in just about a decade and a half. This has lessons for prospective start-up founders in truly innovative spheres. If their venture has to succeed, they must devise 'ways and means' for generating demand as much as for offering supply on a steady basis.

Given these inferences, this study has implications for Flipkart as well as for existing and prospective start-up founders in India. The implications for Flipkart are as follows:

1. The corporate entrepreneurship model developed by Flipkart with a simultaneous focus on supply and demand, which led to its stupendous growth, is unique and worth pursuing further in the long run.
2. Many of the process, market and financial innovations implemented are replicable, as proved by their easy adoption subsequently by competitors, and therefore, there is a constant need to periodically introduce innovations, to continuously enhance demand and match supply in line with that, to be ahead of competitors and remain a 'high growth, high impact' firm in the long run.
3. The entrepreneurial culture in Flipkart is widely perceived as such by Flipsters as much as by ex-Flipsters. A near-unanimous convergence of opinions of management, executives and ex-Flipsters on the 'presence of entrepreneurial culture' is the strongest strength of the company. It needs to be preserved for the successful pursuance of corporate entrepreneurship strategy in the long run.
4. Corporate entrepreneurship is contributed more by proactive, risk-taking and motivated executives who

have higher technical education qualifications than by executives who are entrepreneurial per se. While the former contributed to the growth of the company, the latter might have led to the emergence of a series of tech start-ups from ex-Flipsters outside Flipkart. The former is internally beneficial, whereas the latter is externally beneficial. A 'responsible leader' has to contribute to its ecosystem development along with its growth.

5. Thus, the corporate entrepreneurship strategy along with entrepreneurial culture has contributed to the steady growth of Flipkart as well as to the growth of the entrepreneurial ecosystem, comprising both start-ups and MSMEs, in the country. These contributions are exemplary and worth sustaining.

The implications for existing and prospective start-up founders are as follows:

1. There is a need for a clear 'goal with passion' while ideating and progressing towards the creation of a start-up. A goal-oriented, passionate founder and management are likely to come up with innovations for the success of the start-up.
2. A truly innovative start-up in an evolving ecosystem, in an underdeveloped economy, will face challenges in supply creation as well as demand generation. A simultaneous strategy for supply creation as much as demand generation is key to ensure success in the form of accelerated growth of the new venture in the start-up phase and beyond.
3. Innovations, even if they are replicable, are worth

implementing to reap the immediate benefits of being first movers in the market.

4. In an emerging economy where lower-income groups account for the majority in the consumer market, innovatively meeting their 'consumption aspirations' by converting their desires into demand can be a powerful instrument of growth for e-commerce companies.
5. Nurturing and sustaining entrepreneurial culture among managerial executives are imperative for any enterprise wanting to successfully pursue a corporate entrepreneurship strategy.
6. For a tech start-up, reaping 'economies of scale' need not be the only way for accelerated growth. A combined strategy to reap 'economies of scale' with 'economies of scope' can bring disproportionate benefits for growth.
7. Successfully dealing with M&As can be an effective route for reaping the benefits of 'economies of scope' to achieve inorganic growth for a company.
8. An ambitious company while recruiting talented executives must be prepared to experience periodic attrition of talent which might result in the spring-up of start-ups in the wider ecosystem subsequently. Such start-ups may or may not be beneficial to the company, but they certainly contribute to the ecosystem.
9. Corporate entrepreneurship strategy is not a one-time fixed game; rather, it calls for perseverance, commitment, hard efforts, bold attempts, experiments,

ability to face failures, and skills to raise resources, in a sustainable way for the long term.

10. Corporate entrepreneurship calls for acquiring and nurturing top talent and building an inclusive and innovative people-centric culture.

Future Scope for Research

The present study is confined to the examination of a single start-up-turned-company's growth achievement in the context of corporate entrepreneurship strategy and entrepreneurial culture. Furthermore, the study is largely based on qualitative-cum-quantitative data-based analysis. Given this, there is scope for undertaking a comparative study for two or more start-ups which have grown to become large companies in two or more different ecosystems.

Further primary data (cross-sectional or time series) from a field survey covering a large sample of companies (which have emerged as start-ups), either from a single ecosystem or from multiple ecosystems, would enable robust quantitative analysis, which may bring more rigour with more insights. Finally, there is scope for an exclusive study focussing on a group of scaled-up start-ups to bring out the role and significance of corporate entrepreneurship, for the benefit of policymakers and ecosystem stakeholders.

Future Scope for Research

ACKNOWLEDGEMENTS

The study for *Be Unique, The Flipkart Way: Unravelling Unprecedented Corporate Entrepreneurship* was conducted collaboratively by us from June 2021 to December 2022. While the original idea was Varadharaju Janardhanan's, it was conceptualized by M.H. Bala Subrahmanya, and later developed by both of us. In the course of the study, we received unstinted support from both within Flipkart and outside, and we deem it appropriate to acknowledge the help we received from one and all.

Kalyan Krishnamurthy, CEO, Flipkart, made time for an extended interaction-cum-interview in which he shed light on issues concerning Flipkart's growth, its vision and mission, the challenges the organization dealt with in the process of its rapid growth and while promoting entrepreneurial culture and corporate entrepreneurship. All this despite his packed schedule. We are greatly indebted to him for his support and encouragement.

Binny Bansal, co-founder, Flipkart, was extremely generous and spontaneous in his answers to our questions on the challenges he faced from the inception of Flipkart in 2007 till 2022. He described in great detail some critical issues concerning Flipkart—its purpose and mission, its transformation from time to time since its birth to becoming first a unicorn, then a decacorn, its takeover by Walmart, and its unprecedented growth story over time, including the promotion of entrepreneurial culture and corporate entrepreneurship, among others.

Krishna Raghavan was extremely supportive and encouraging of this study from the beginning. He also shared with us his perspective on Flipkart's journey since its inception.

Key senior-level executives of Flipkart, including intrapreneurs and founders of start-ups taken over by Flipkart, were kind enough to make time for individual interviews to share their personal experiences of Flipkart's growth story. These interviews have greatly contributed to this study. We thank them individually and collectively.

As part of this study, we interviewed and interacted with 22 start-up founders who were ex-Flipsters. They had served Flipkart in diverse functional areas and verticals at different levels of the hierarchy, and after gathering years of experience, exposure, networking, etc., they quit Flipkart to start their own ventures at different points in time between 2007 and 2022. Each founder spent quality time sharing their experiences, both during their stint at Flipkart and after. It was evident that directly or indirectly, Flipkart had played a crucial role in enabling them to start their new ventures. We are indeed grateful to each founder/co-founder for sparing their valuable time and enlightening us as much about Flipkart as about their own start-ups.

Based on a semi-structured questionnaire, we gathered

primary data from 50 Flipkart executives serving in different verticals at different levels of the hierarchy. Each one provided answers to all the questions, thereby contributing immensely on the measure of corporate entrepreneurship currently prevalent in Flipkart and its determinants. We thank them individually and collectively.

Strafford Joe Fernandes, Sheetal Singh and Ishmeet Dang supported us from the very inception of this study until its completion by providing insightful feedback on the manuscript. They also facilitated interviews and interactions with various participants mentioned earlier in this section. Without their help, it would have been difficult to complete this study. We are truly grateful to them.

Anantha Padmanabha, System Administrator, Department of Management Studies, Indian Institute of Science, Bangalore, helped us prepare and revise the study and later format the draft report. We deeply appreciate his support.

Rupa Publications and Dibakar Ghosh for being our excellent publishing partners and helping enhance the reach of our work, and more importantly, bringing this unique research to life.

Finally, we thank all those who may not have been mentioned here, but who directly or indirectly facilitated and supported the book from its inception to its final avatar—*Be Unique, The Flipkart Way.*

Varadharaju Janardhanan and
M.H. Bala Subrahmanya
July 2024
Bengaluru, India

BIBLIOGRAPHY

Abrar, P. (2022): 'Flipkart launches Leap Ahead and Leap Innovation Network start-up programmes', *Business Standard*, January 17. https://www.business-standard.com/article/companies/flipkart-launches-leap-ahead-and-leap-innovation-network-start-up-programmes-122011700860_1.html.

Accessed on 20 April 2022.

Abrar, P. (2021): 'Flipkart launches Shopsy to enable over 25 million online entrepreneurs by 2023', *Business Standard*, July 2. https://www.business-standard.com/article/companies/flipkart-launches-shopsy-to-enable-over-25-mn-online-entrepreneurs-by-2023-121070100939_1.html. Accessed on 12 April 2022.

Acs, Z.J., P. Braunerjelm, D.B. Auretsch, and B. Carlsson (2009): 'The Knowledge Spillover Theory of Entrepreneurship', *Small Business Economics*, 32: 15–30.

Agarwal, N. (2018): 'Flipkart launches 2GUD, new e-commerce portal for refurbished goods'. https://www.livemint.com/Companies/vzRSAgDD9LT11k1IWamh1J/Flipkart-launches-2GUD-ecommerce-portal-refurbished-goods.html.

Ahmed, M. (2017): 'Flipkart's US-based innovation lab is building AI products to engage with customers', *Techradar*, June 30.

https://www.techradar.com/in/news/how-flipkarts-f7-labs-is-building-ai-products-to-engage-with-customers. Accessed on 10 March 2022.

Ambad, S.N.A., and K.A. Wahab (2016): 'The Relationship between Corporate Entrepreneurship and Firm Performance: Evidence from Malaysian Large Companies', *International Journal of Business and Society*, 17 (2), 259–280.

Amo, B.W. (2010): 'Corporate Entrepreneurship and Intrapreneurship Related to Innovation Behavior among Employees', *International Journal of Entrepreneurial Venturing*, 2 (2), 144–158.

Antoncic, B., and R.D. Hisrich (2003): 'Clarifying the Intrapreneurship Concept', *Journal of Small Business and Enterprise Development*, 10 (1), 7–24.

Arakali, H. (2018): 'Flipkart acquires mobile repair shop chain F1 Info Solutions to boost after-sales capabilities', *India Forbes*, September 26. https://www.forbesindia.com/article/special/flipkart-acquires-mobile-repair-shop-chain-f1-info-solutions-to-boost-aftersales-capabilities/48259/1. Accessed on 30 March 2022.

Audretsch, D.B. (2012): 'Determinants of High-Growth Entrepreneurship', Report prepared for the OECD/DBA International Workshop on 'High-growth firms: Local policies and local determinants', Copenhagen, 28 March 2012.

Bala Subrahmanya, M.H. (2018): 'How Distinct are Technology-based Start-ups in India? Features, Policies and Evolving Ecosystems', *Asian Journal of Innovation and Policy*, 7 (1), 30–54.

Bala Subrahmanya, M.H. (2022): 'Competitiveness of High-Tech Start-ups and Entrepreneurial Ecosystems: An Overview',

JGBC, 17 (1), 1–10. https://doi.org/10.1007/s42943-022-00056-w.

Bala Subrahmanya, M.H. (2021): *Entrepreneurial Ecosystems for Tech Start-ups in India: Evolution, Structure and Role*, De Gruyter, Berlin, Germany.

Bala Subrahmanya, M.H. (2020): 'Entrepreneurial Ecosystem for Tech Start-ups in Bangalore: An Exploration of Structure and Gap', *Journal of Small Business and Enterprise Development*, 27 (7), 1167–1185.

Bala Subrahmanya, M.H. (2017): 'How Did Bangalore Emerge as One of the Global Start-up Hubs in India: Entrepreneurial Ecosystem – Emergence, Structure and Role', *Journal of Developmental Entrepreneurship*, 22 (1), March, 22 pages.

Banerjee, A. (2017): 'Flipkart's "buyback guarantee" offer: Why it's a boon for smartphone users', *Business Standard*, May 12. https://www.business-standard.com/article/companies/flipkart-s-buyback-guarantee-offer-why-it-s-a-boon-for-smartphone-users-117051200472_1.html. Accessed on 22 March 2022.

Banerjee, Sayed – Start-up Talky (2022): 'List of 111 Unicorn Start-ups in India and Counting | 2024 Updated'. https://start-uptalky.com/top-unicorn-start-ups-india/.

Bansal, V. (2019): 'Exclusive: Flipkart acquires a 20% stake in loyalty management start-up EasyRewardz', *Entracker*, November 19. https://entrackr.com/2019/11/exclusive-flipkart-acquire-stake-easyrewardz/. Accessed on 6 April 2022.

Barringer, B.R., and A.C. Bluedorn (1999): 'The Relationship between Corporate Entrepreneurship and Strategic Management', *Strategic Management Journal*, 20, 421–444.

BGR.in (2016): 'Flipkart's logistic arm Ekart launches courier service', News item, May 20. https://www.bgr.in/news/

flipkarts-logistics-arm-ekart-launches-courier-service-404804/. Accessed on 12 March 2022.

Bidkar, C. (2017): 'Flipkart's F7 Labs focuses on building artificial intelligence-based products'. https://techstory.in/flipkart-artificial-intelligence-0106/.

Bierwerth, M., C. Schwens, R. Isidor, and R. Kabst (2015): 'Corporate Entrepreneurship and Performance: A Meta-Analysis', *Small Business Economics*, 45: 255–278.

Bouchard, V., and A. Fayolle (2018): *Corporate Entrepreneurship*, Routledge, Taylor & Francis Group, London.

Burgelman, R.A. (1984): 'Designs for Corporate Entrepreneurship in Established Firms', *California Management Review*, 26 (3), 154–166.

Burns, P. (2013): *Corporate Entrepreneurship: Innovation and Strategy in Large Organizations*, Palgrave Macmillan, New York.

Burns, P. (2008): *Corporate Entrepreneurship: Building the Entrepreneurial Organization*, Third edition, Palgrave Macmillan, New York.

Business Connect (2021): 'The success story of Flipkart, how India's first e-commerce company started', blog, September 20. https://businessconnectindia.in/the-success-story-of-flipkart/#:~:text=Flipkart%20was%20founded%20by%20Sachin,to%20the%20creation%20of%20Flipkart. Accessed on 21 January 2022.

Business Standard (2022): 'Flipkart acquires ANS Commerce to strengthen its e-commerce ecosystem', April 19. https://www.business-standard.com/article/companies/flipkart-acquires-ans-commerce-to-strengthen-its-e-commerce-ecosystem-122041900619_1.html. Accessed on 21 April 2022.

Business Standard, New Delhi (2023): 'No mass layoffs are

happening at company: Chief People Officer, Flipkart'. https://www.gfmreview.com/index.php/banking/no-mass-layoffs-are-happening-at-company-chief-people-officer-flipkart.

Business Standard (2018): 'Flipkart launches independent 2GUD platform for refurbished', August 22, Bengaluru.

Calvino, F., C. Criscuolo, and C. Menon (2015): 'Cross-Country Evidence on Start-Up Dynamics', OECD Science, Technology and Industry Working Papers, No. 2015/06, OECD Publishing, Paris.

Chakraborty, S. (2017): 'The Flipkart story: A timeline of funding from 2007 to 2017', *Financial Express*, March 20. https://www.financialexpress.com/industry/technology/the-flipkart-story-a-timeline-of-funding-from-2007-to-2017/595740/. Accessed on 16 February 2022.

Chanchani, M., and S. Dave (2015): 'Flipkart picking up 34% stake in digital mapping firm MapmyIndia in Rs. 1600 crore deal', *The Economic Times*, December 4. https://economictimes.indiatimes.com/small-biz/start-ups/flipkart-picking-up-34-stake-in-digital-mapping-firm-mapmyindia-in-rs-1600-crore-deal/articleshow/50034934.cms?from=mdr. Accessed on 12 March 2022.

Chanchani-ET CIO,2017: 'Kalyan Krishnamurthy to be Flipkart's new CEO'. https://cio.economictimes.indiatimes.com/news/strategy-and-management/kalyan-krishnamurthy-to-be-flipkarts-new-ceo-sachin-bansal-to-remain-group-chairman/56434678#:~:text=Strategy%20and%20Management-,Kalyan%20Krishnamurthy%20to%20be%20Flipkart's%20new%20CEO%3B%20Sachin%20Bansal%20to,to%20remain%20as%20group%20chairman.

Chathurvedula, S. (2016): 'Flipkart acquires UPI-based payments start-up PhonePe', *Mint*, April 04. https://www.livemint.com/Companies/DbMTb2tDKuZoTfEa203XBL/Flipkart-acquires-UPIbased-payments-start-up-PhonePe.html. Accessed on 12 March 2022.

Coad, A., S.O. Daunfeldt, W. Holzl, D. Johansson, and P. Nightingale (2014): 'High-Growth Firms: Introduction to the Special Section', *Industrial and Corporate Change*, 23 (1), 91–112.

Corbett, A., J.G. Covin, G.C. O'Connor, and C.L. Tucci (2013): 'Corporate Entrepreneurship: State-of-the-Art Research and a Future Research Agenda', *Journal of Product Innovation Management*, 30 (5), 812–820.

Covin, J.G., and M.P. Miles (1999): 'Corporate Entrepreneurship and the Pursuit of Competitive Advantage', *Entrepreneurship Theory and Practice*, 23 (3), 47–63.

Dalal, M. (2019): 'The untold story of Flipkart, the big billion ecommerce start-up', Expert Opinion, *Your Story*, October 8. https://yourstory.com/2019/10/flipkart-story-big-billion-start-up-ecommerce

Crunchbase Flipkart Series F, G, H: **Crunchbase Series H,** https://www.crunchbase.com/funding_round/flipkart-series-h--fc494b83. **Crunchbase Series F,** https://www.crunchbase.com/funding_round/flipkart-series-f--425583e2. **Crunchbase Series G,** https://www.crunchbase.com/funding_round/flipkart-series-g--30ae57bd.

Crunchbase (2021): 'The Year of the Decacorn'. https://news.crunchbase.com/venture/decacorn-start-ups-2021-global-record-data-charts/.

Crunchbase: 'Flipkart Company Financials'. https://www.crunchbase.com/organization/flipkart/company_financials.

Crunchbase Series B: 'Funding Round Series B – Flipkart'.

https://www.crunchbase.com/funding_round/flipkart-series-b--c3ab876c.

Crunchbase, Series C: https://www.crunchbase.com/funding_round/flipkart-series-c--88641577.

Dalal, M. (2014): 'Flipkart enters strategic partnership with Jeeves Consumer', *Mint*, November 07. https://www.livemint.com/Companies/NHrrYYszDGsHenizUKolWJ/Flipkart-enters-strategic-partnership-with-Jeeves-Consumer.html. Accessed on 22 February 2022.

Dalal, M. (2015): 'Flipkart close to third acquisition this year'. https://www.livemint.com/Companies/xVzeDSgcklGk8ipgAUf0GJ/Flipkart-close-to-third-acquisition-this-year.html.

Dalal, M., and S. Anirban (2018): 'Ashish Gupta, the angel who struck gold in Flipkart sale to Walmart', 11 May. https://www.livemint.com/Companies/J25VyjJIhvYZ8o7a5EMr0J/Ashish-Gupta-the-angel-who-struck-gold-in-Flipkart-sale-to.html. Accessed on 10 February 2022.

Dalal, M. (2019b): *Big Billion Start-up: The Untold Flipkart Story*, Macmillan, New Delhi.

Danish, R., J. Asghar, Z. Ahmad, and H.F. Ali (2019): 'Factors Affecting "Entrepreneurial Culture": The Mediating Role of Creativity', *Journal of Innovation and Entrepreneurship*, 8 (14). https://doi.org/10/1186/s13731-019-0108-9.

Davidsson, P. (2015): 'Entrepreneurial Opportunities and the Entrepreneurship Nexus: A Re-Conceptualization', *Journal of Business Venturing*, 30 (5), 674–695.

Davies, P. (2022): 'VivaTech 2022: What could Europe learn from India's tech minister and its strong start-up scene?', euronews.next. https://www.euronews.com/next/2022/06/17/vivatech-2022-what-could-europe-learn-from-indias-tech-minister-

and-its-strong-start-up-sc. Accessed on 17 June 2022.

de Jong, J.P.J., S.K. Parker, S. Wennekers, and C. Wu (2011): 'Corporate Entrepreneurship at the Individual Level: Measurement and Determinants', EIM Research Report – H201108, Zoetermeer, The Netherlands.

Department of Industrial Policy and Promotion (2016): *Start-up India Action Plan*, Government of India, New Delhi.

Dess, G.G., R.D. Ireland, S.A. Zahra, S.W. Floyd, J.J. Janney, and P.J. Lane (2003): 'Emerging Issues in Corporate Entrepreneurship', *Journal of Management*, 29 (3), 351–378.

Dighe, S. (2022): http://www.sandeepdighe.com/flipkart.html. Accessed on 23 March 2022.

Divekar, A. (2014): 'Flipkart in partnership with Motorola to launch Moto G Smartphones', *Business Standard*, February 6. https://www.business-standard.com/article/companies/flipkart-in-partnership-with-motorola-to-launch-moto-g-smartphones-114020500799_1.html. Accessed on 26 February 2022.

DT Next (2020): 'Motorola partners with Flipkart to launch smart home appliances', October 9. https://www.dtnext.in/business/2020/10/09/motorola-partners-with-flipkart-to-launch-smart-home-appliances. Accessed on 6 March 2022.

Dutta, D.K. (2018): 'In Competition with Oneself: A Qualitative Inquiry into Amazon's Entrepreneurial Culture', *Technology Innovation Management Review*, 8 (6), 5–14.

EasyRewardz: Flipkart puts $4 million in Easyrewardz. https://www.easyrewardz.com/flipkart-puts-4-million-in-easyrewardz/

EazyRewardz Corp: Flipkart puts $4 million in Easyrewardz.

https://www.easyrewardz.com/flipkart-puts-4-million-in-easyrewardz/.

Ederer, F., and S. Ma (2018): 'Do Companies Buy Competitors in Order to Shut Them Down?', *Yale Insights*. https://insights.som.yale.edu/insights/do-companies-buy-competitors-in-order-to-shut-them-down, Accessed on 24 October 2022.

Elahi, B. (2018): *Safety Risk Management for Medical Devices*, Academic Press, ISBN 978-0-12-813098-8.

Eshwar, B. (2015): 'Flipkart launches new mobile site, Flipkart Lite', *OfficeChai*, November 9. https://officechai.com/news/flipkart-lite/. Accessed on 8 March 2022.

ET Bureau (2018): 'Walmart acquires Flipkart for $16 billion in world's largest ecommerce deal', *The Economic Times*, May 10. https://economictimes.indiatimes.com/small-biz/start-ups/newsbuzz/walmart-acquires-flipkart-for-16-bn-worlds-largest-ecommerce-deal/articleshow/64095145.cms. Accessed on 31 March 2022.

ETtech (2022): 'Flipkart group acquires electronics recommerce platform Yaantra for $40 million', *The Economic Times*, January 13. https://economictimes.indiatimes.com/tech/funding/flipkart-group-acquires-electronics-recommerce-platform-yaantra-for-40-million/articleshow/88879726.cms. Accessed on 12 April 2022.

ETtech (2021): 'Flipkart expands 90-min delivery service Quick to six new cities'. https://economictimes.indiatimes.com/tech/technology/flipkart-expands-90-min-delivery-service-quick-to-six-new-cities/articleshow/82159844.cms?from=mdr.

ETtech (2021): 'Flipkart acquires Cleartrip as part of its diversification drive', *The Economic Times*, April 15. https://economictimes.indiatimes.com/tech/start-ups/flipkart-acquires-cleartrip-as-part-of-its-diversification-drive/articleshow/82082840.cms?from=mdr. Accessed on 10 April 2022.

European Commission (2007): *Eurostat – OECD Manual on Business Demography Statistics*, European Commission, Luxembourg.

Farinos, J.E., B. Herrero, and M.A. Lattore (2011): 'Corporate Entrepreneurship and Acquisitions: Creating Firm Wealth', *International Entrepreneurship and Management Journal*, 7: 325–339.

Fini, R., R. Grimaldi, G.L. Marzocchi, and M. Sobrero (2012): 'The Determinants of Corporate Entrepreneurial Intention within Small and Newly Established Firms', *Entrepreneurship Theory and Practice*, 36 (2), 193–203.

Firstpost (2018): 'Flipkart to shutter Flyte music service due to piracy, micro-payment issues'. https://www.firstpost.com/tech/news-analysis/flipkart-to-shutter-flyte-music-service-due-to-piracy-micro-payment-issues-2-3627369.html.

Flipkart Brands: https://brands.flipkart.com/catapult-about.

Flipkart Corporate: Flipkart Group Companies: https://corporate.flipkart.net/group.

Flipkart Leap: https://www.flipkartleap.com.

Flipkart Pay Later: 'Frequently Asked Questions: Flipkart Pay Later'. https://www.flipkart.com/pages/paylater-main-tnc.

Flipkart Stories, Announcements (2018): Newsroom Announcements. https://stories.flipkart.com/announcements/#aug-2018.

Flipkart Stories (2017): 'Debit Card EMI from Flipkart – Here's everything you need to know', October 16. https://stories.flipkart.com/debit-card-emi/. Accessed on 24 March 2022.

Flipkart Stories (2018): 'Flipkart's Complete Mobile Protection –

it's like insurance for your mobile phone', October 8. https://stories.flipkart.com/complete-mobile-protection/. Accessed on 26 March 2022.

Flipkart Stories (2019): 'Flipkart launches "Samarth" to empower Indian artisans, weavers and craftsmen'. https://stories.flipkart.com/flipkart-samarth-indian-artisans-weavers-craftsmen/. Accessed on 20 April 2022.

Flipkart Stories (2022): 'Flipkart onboards gaming start-up Mech Mocha to strengthen its gaming strategy'. https://stories.flipkart.com/201102-mech-mocha-pr-rev_final/.

Flipkart Stories, Timeline: 'The Flipkart Timeline'. https://stories.flipkart.com/flipkart-timeline-milestones/.

Flipkart Stories: 'From fashion in the metaverse to insurtech, Flipkart Leap Ahead finalists are innovating for India!'. https://stories.flipkart.com/flipkart-leap-ahead-cohort-finalists/.

Flipkart Leap Press Release (2020): '"Flipkart Leap comes at an opportune time for the Indian start-up ecosystem" – Q&A with Naren Ravula'. https://stories.flipkart.com/flipkart-leap-start-up-accelerator-naren-ravula/.

Flipkart Press Release (FKH+) (2021): 'Flipkart to enter the healthcare sector through Flipkart Health+, aims to provide consumers access to affordable and convenient healthcare'. .https://storiesflistgv2.blob.core.windows.net/stories/2021/11/Final-Flipkart-Health-Press-Release.docx.pdf.

Flipkart Press Release (2018): 'Flipkart launches 2GUD'. https://storiesflistgv2.blob.core.windows.net/stories/2019/11/5dc117e2b0c10-5dc117e2b0c16Flipkart-launches-2GUD-a-new-e-commerce-value-platform-for-refurbished-goods.pdf.pdf.

Flipkart Press Release (2022): 'Flipkart Group acquires electronics recommerce company Yaantra'. https://storiesflistgv2.blob.core.windows.net/stories/2022/01/FINAL-220113-Flipkart-Group-acquires-electronics-recommerce-company-Yaantra.pdf.

Flipkart Press release (2021): 'Flipkart announces finalists of its first-ever start-up accelerator

program Flipkart Leap'. https://storiesflistgv2.blob.core.windows.net/stories/2021/01/FINAL-Press-Release_-Flipkart-announces-finalists-of-its-first-ever-start-up-accelerator-program-Flipkart-Leap.docx.pdf.

Flipkart Press Release (2021b): 'Flipkart Leap Demo Day: Eight Start-ups Showcase Their Futuristic Technologies To Innovate For India'. https://storiesflistgv2.blob.core.windows.net/stories/2021/07/FINAL-Press-Release_-Flipkart-Leap-Demo-Day_-Eight-Start-ups-Showcase-Their-Futuristic-Technologies-To-Innovate-For-India.pdf.

Flipkart Ventures: https://ventures.flipkart.com/about.

Flipkart Press Release, Leap 2021 (b): 'Flipkart Leap Demo Day: Eight Start-ups Showcase Their Futuristic Technologies To Innovate For India'. https://storiesflistgv2.blob.core.windows.net/stories/2021/11/FINAL-Press-Release_-Flipkart-Leap-Demo-Day_-Eight-Start-ups-Showcase-Their-Futuristic-Technologies-To-Innovate-For-India.pdf.

Flipkart Stories, Press Release: https://storiesflistgv2.blob.core.windows.net/stories/2020/07/200709-Press-release-Flipkart-AFL-vf.pdf.

Arvind Fashions Press Release: https://www.arvindfashions.com/wp-content/uploads/2022/03/41-Strategic-Partnership-Announcement-with-FK-09-07-2020.pdf.

Flipkart Press Release, Leap 2022: 'Flipkart Leap opens

applications for cohort 2 of its flagship start-up program; launches Flipkart Leap Ahead and Flipkart Leap Innovation Network'. https://storiesflistgv2.blob.core.windows.net/stories/2022/01/17012022-Flipkart-Leap-opens-applications-for-cohort-2-of-its-start-up-program.pdf.

Fowler, G., and A. Monteiro (2018): 'High-Growth Firms and Scale-Ups: A Review and Research Agenda', *RAUSP Management Journal*, 54 (1), 96–111.

Gai, B., and B. Joffe (2013): *India Start-up Report*, World Start-up Report. www.worldstartpreport.com.

Garica-Morales, V.J., M.T. Bolivar-Ramos, and R. Martin-Rojas (2014): 'Technological Variables and Absorptive Capacity's Influence on Performance through Corporate Entrepreneurship', *Journal of Business Research*, 67, 1468–1477.

Gautam, V., and V. Verma (1997): 'Corporate Entrepreneurship: Changing Perspectives', *Journal of Entrepreneurship*, 6 (2), 233–242.

Genç, K.Y. (2012): 'The Response of the Entrepreneurship to the Changing Business Environment: Strategic Entrepreneurship', *International Journal of Economic and Administrative Studies, 5* (9), 71–83.

Ghoshal, A. (2018): 'Flipkart to invest $25 mn in Silicon Valley start-ups to ramp up deep-tech play'. https://www.techcircle.in/2018/02/06/flipkart-to-invest-25-mn-in-silicon-valley-start-ups-to-ramp-up-deep-tech-play.

Glinyanova, M., R.B. Bouncken, V. Tiberius, and A.C.C. Ballester (2021): 'Five Decades of Corporate Entrepreneurship Research: Measuring and Mapping the Field', *International Entrepreneurship and Management Journal*, 17: 1731–1757.

Govindayapalli, M. (2020): 'Creating the butterfly effect in Indian startup ecosystem'. https://thestrategystory.com/2020/12/11/flipsters-creating-butterfly-effect/

Gupta, D. (2017): 'Kalyan Krishnamurthy appointed as new CEO of Flipkart, replaces Binny Bansal, other top positions reshuffled too', *India.com*, January 11. https://www.india.com/technology/kalyan-krishnamurthy-appointed-as-new-ceo-of-flipkart-other-top-positions-reshuffled-too-1749626/. Accessed on 24 March 2022.

Hair, J.F., W.C. Black, B.J. Babin, R.E. Anderson, and R.L. Tatham (2007): *Multivariate Data Analysis,* Dorling Kindersley (India) Private Limited, New Delhi.

Hamel, G. (2002): *Leading the Revolution: How to Thrive in Turbulent Times by Making Innovation a Way of Life*. Boston: Harvard Business School Press.

Hayton, J.C., and D.J. Kelley (2006): 'A Competency-Based Framework for Promoting Corporate Entrepreneurship', *Human Resource Management*, 45 (3), 407–427.

Hector, D.T. (2018): 'Flipkart acquires Israeli analytics start-up Upstream Commerce', *VCCircle*, September 25. https://www.vccircle.com/flipkart-acquires-israeli-analytics-start-up-upstream-commerce. Accessed on 4 April 2022.

Hisrick, R.D., and C. Kearney (2012): *Corporate Entrepreneurship: How to Create a Thriving Entrepreneurial Spirit Throughout Your Company*, McGraw Hill, New York.

Hossan, S. (2021): 'The History and Rise of Flipkart: Largest eCommerce Company in India'. https://businessinspection.com.bd/history-and-rise-of-flipkart/.

Howarth, J. (2022): 'What percentage of start-ups fail?', https://explodingtopics.com/blog/start-up-failure-stats. Accessed on 26 October 2022.

IANS (2022): 'Flipkart acquires e-commerce start-up ANS Commerce'. https://timesofindia.indiatimes.com/business/start-ups/companies/flipkart-acquires-e-commerce-start-up-ans-commerce/articleshow/90935911.cms.

India Briefing (2022): 'India's unicorn start-ups: Sector distribution, funding and global profile'. https://www.india-briefing.com/news/indias-unicorn-start-ups-sector-distribution-funding-ecosystem-global-comparison-25104.html/. Accessed on 15 July 2022.

Inc42 (2015): 'Flipkart acquires payment services start-up FX Mart for about $6.8 mn'.

https://inc42.com/flash-feed/flipkart-acquires-payment-services-start-up-fx-mart-for-about-6-8-mn/#:~:text=FX%20Mart%20was%20started%20in,to%20the%20external%20wallet%20providers.

India TV News (2018): 'Flipkart's journey: From start-up worth Rs 4 lakh in 2007 to e-commerce giant valued at Rs 1.47 lakh crore in 2018 | Here's all you need to know'. https://www.indiatvnews.com/business/news-flipkart-s-journey-from-start-up-worth-rs-4-lakh-in-2007-to-e-commerce-giant-valued-at-rs-1-47-lakh-crore-in-2018-here-s-all-you-need-to-know-441587

Invest India (2022): 'The Indian Unicorn Landscape'. https://www.investindia.gov.in/indian-unicorn-landscape. Accessed on 15 July 2022.

Ireland, D.R., D.F. Kuratko, and J.G. Covin (2017): 'Antecedents, Elements, and Consequences of Corporate Entrepreneurship Strategy', *Academy of Management Proceedings*, 2003 (1), L1–L6.

Ireland, D.R., J.G. Covin, and D.F. Kuratko (2009): 'Conceptualizing Corporate Entrepreneurship Strategy', *Entrepreneurship Theory and Practice*, 33 (1), 19–46.

Ireland, R.D., D.F. Kuratko, and M.H. Morris (2006): 'A Health Audit for Corporate Entrepreneurship: Innovation at All Levels', Part I, *Journal of Business Strategy*, 27 (1), 10–17.

Ireland, R.D., M.A. Hitt, and D.G. Sirmon (2003): 'A Model of Strategic Entrepreneurship: The Construct and its Dimensions', *Journal of Management*, 29 (6), 963–989.

Isi, C. (2019): 'Flipkart launches credit card in association with Axis Bank, offers %5 cashback on purchases', *mysmartprice*, July 11. https://www.mysmartprice.com/gear/flipkart-launches-credit-card-association-axis-bank-offers-5-cashback-purchases/. Accessed on 4 April 2022.

ITVoice (2022): 'Flipkart invests in logistics start-up Zinka'. https://www.itvoice.in/flipkart-invests-in-logistics-start-up-zinka. Accessed on 10 March 2022.

Jayadevan, P.K. (2016): '6 charts that tell you about Flipkart's growth'. https://archive.factordaily.com/flipkart-revenue-profit-2015/#:~:text=In%20FY2015%2C%20Flipkart%20Ltd%20clocked,to%20%2D25.21%25%20in%20FY2015.

Jayadevan, P.K. (2016): 'Flipkart's losses pile up but revenue grows 50%'. https://archive.factordaily.com/flipkart-revenue-profit-loss-2016/.

Juvanovic, B. (1982): 'Selection and the Evolution of Industry', *Econometrica*, 50 (3), 649–670.

Keshavdev, V. (2021): 'Idea of cash on delivery was a major innovation', *Fortune India*, October 8. https://www.fortuneindia.com/venture/idea-of-cash-on-delivery-was-a-major-innovation/105984. Accessed on 10 February 2022.

Khatri, B. (2018): 'Flipkart decides to shutdown Ebay.in, to launch its own refurbished goods platform'. *Inc42*, July 24. https://

inc42.com/buzz/flipkart-decides-to-shut-down-ebay-in-to-launch-its-own-refurbished-platform/. Accessed on 24 March 2022.

Khatri, B. (2018): 'Flipkart losses soar by 68% despite 29% growth in revenue for FY17'. https://inc42.com/buzz/flipkart-revenue-loss-fy17/#:~:text=The%20company%20has%20reportedly%20registered,which%20ended%20in%20March%202017.

King, D.R., S. Schriber, F. Bauer, and S. Amiri (2018): 'Acquisitions as Corporate Entrepreneurship', S. Finkelstein and C.L. Cooper (eds.), *Advances in Mergers and Acquisitions, Vol. 17*, Emerald Publishing Limited, Bingley, pp. 119–144. https://doi.org/10.1108/S1479-361X20180000017006.

Korashev, K. (2022): 'Start-up failure rate: How many start-ups fail and why?', *Failory*, updated on 9 January 2022. https://www.failory.com/blog/start-up-failure-rate. Accessed on 11 July 2022.

Kreiser, P.M., D.F. Kuratko, J.G. Covin, R.D. Ireland, and J.S. Hornsby (2021): 'Corporate Entrepreneurship Strategy: Extending Our Knowledge Boundaries through Configuration Theory', *Small Business Economics*, 56: 739–758.

Kritikos, A.S. (2014): 'Entrepreneurs and Their Impact on Jobs and Economic Growth', IZA World of Labor, 2014: 8. Doi:10.15185/izawol.8.

Kuratko, D.F., and M.H. Morris (2018): 'Corporate Entrepreneurship: A Critical Challenge for Educators and Researchers', *Entrepreneurship Education and Pedagogy*.

Kuratko, D.F., J.S., Hornsby, and J. Hayton (2015): 'Corporate Entrepreneurship: The Innovative Challenge for a New Global Economic Reality', *Small Business Economics*, 45: 245–253.

Kuratko, D.F., J.S. Hornsby, and J.G. Covin (2014): 'Diagnosing a

Firm's Internal Environment for Corporate Entrepreneurship', *Business Horizons*, 57, 37–47.

Kuratko, D.F., and D.B. Audretsch (2013): 'Clarifying the Domains of Corporate Entrepreneurship', *International Entrepreneurship Management Journal*, 9: 323–335.

Kuratko, D.F., R.D. Ireland, and J.S. Hornsby (2004): 'Corporate Entrepreneurship Behavior among Managers: A Review of Theory, Research and Practice', *Advances in Entrepreneurship, Firm Emergence and Growth*, Emerald Group Publishing Limited, Bingley, 7–45. https://doi.org/10.1016/S1074-7540(04)07002-3.

Kuratko, D.F., R.D. Ireland, and J.S. Hornsby (2001): 'Improving Firm Performance through Entrepreneurial Actions: Acordia's Corporate Entrepreneurship Strategy', *Academy of Management Perspectives*, 15(4). https://doi.org/10.5465/ame.2001.5897658.

Laskar, A (2020): 'Walmart readies for $10 billion Flipkart IPO', *Mint*, 7 December.

Lattacher, W., P. Gregori, P. Holzman, and E.J. Schwarz (2021): 'Knowledge Spillover in Entrepreneurial Emergence: A Learning Perspective', *Technological Forecasting & Social Change*, 166: 1–13.

Lee, S.M., and M. Peterson (2000): 'Culture, Entrepreneurial Orientation and Global Competitiveness', *Journal of World Business*, 35, 401–416.

Lewis, M. (2007): 'Stepwise versus Hierarchical Regression: Pros and Cons'. Paper presented at the *Annual Meeting of the Southwest Educational Research Association*, 7 February 2007, San Antonio.

Lockhead, M. (2008): 'In My Opinion', *Management Today*, 2008.

MapmyIndia Press Release, 2015: 'Flipkart acquires strategic minority stake in MapmyIndia'. https://www.mapmyindia.com/downloads/press-release/Press-Release-Flipkart-invests-in-MapmyIndia.pdf.

Maxwell, J.A. (1996): *Qualitative Research Design: An Interactive Approach*, Sage Publications, London.

Medianama (2013): 'Flipkart sells front end ops to former Onmobile COO & others: Report'. https://www.medianama.com/2013/02/223-flipkart-ws-retail-rajiv-kuchhal/. Accessed on 15 July 2022.

Mendonca (2017): 'Flipkart focuses on AI-based products to grow its presence in Silicon Valley'.

https://economictimes.indiatimes.com/small-biz/security-tech/technology/flipkart-focuses-on-ai-based-products-to-grow-its-presence-in-silicon-valley/articleshow/58938498.cms?from=mdr.

Mehta, J (2013): 'Flipkart launches its online payment solution – PayZippy', September 5, *Your Story*. https://yourstory.com/2013/07/flipkart-launches-its-online-payment-solution-payzippy/amp. Accessed on 24 February 2022.

Menon, M. (2016): 'The inspiring story behind Flipkart', *MW*. https://www.mansworldindia.com/people/19530/. Accessed on 14 February 2022.

Miller, D. (1983): 'The Correlates of Entrepreneurship in Three Types of Firms', *Management Science*, 29 (7), 770–791.

Ministry of MSMEs (2013): *Recommendations of the Inter-Ministerial Committee for Accelerating Manufacturing in Micro, Small and Medium Enterprises Sector*, Government of India, New Delhi.

Mint (2020a): 'Flipkart launches accelerator program "Flipkart Leap"', August 10. https://www.livemint.com/companies/

start-ups/flipkart-launches-start-up-accelerator-program-flipkart-leap-11597040928084.html. Accessed on 6 April 2022.

Mint (2020b): 'Flipkart launches 90-minute delivery service', July 28. https://www.livemint.com/companies/news/flipkart-launches-90-minute-delivery-service-11595919001189.html. Accessed on 8 April 2022.

Mint (2020c): 'Flipkart Group acquires AR start-up Scapic with eye on immersive shopping', November 17. https://www.livemint.com/companies/news/flipkart-group-acquires-gaming-start-up-scapic-with-eye-on-immersive-shopping-11605590761065.html. Accessed on 12 April 2022.

Moneycontrol (2019): 'Flipkart launches venture fund to invest in e-commerce, fin-tech start-ups', March 26. https://www.moneycontrol.com/news/business/flipkart-launches-venture-fund-to-invest-in-e-commerce-fin-tech-start-ups-3704301.html. Accessed on 4 April 2022.

Moneycontrol (2018): 'Flipkart betting big on artificial intelligence to improve core functions', *Moneycontrol News*, April 5. https://www.moneycontrol.com/news/business/start-up/flipkart-betting-big-on-artificial-intelligence-to-improve-core-functions-2543337.html. Accessed on 10 March 2022.

Mookerji, N. (2013): 'Flipkart aims for 10-fold growth in revenue in FY12'. https://www.business-standard.com/article/companies/flipkart-aims-for-10-fold-growth-in-revenue-in-fy12-111122700025_1.html.

Nair, A. (2016): 'Flipkart now offers no-cost EMI, but how viable are the financing options for e-buyers?', *Your Story*, April 8. https://yourstory.com/2016/06/flipkart-no_cost-emi/amp. Accessed on 20 March 2022.

Nason, R.S., A. McKelvie, and G.T. Lumpkin (2015): 'The Role of

Organizational Size in the Heterogeneous Nature of Corporate Entrepreneurship', *Small Business Economics*, 45: 279–304.

NDTV Profit, PTI (2023): 'Flipkart tightens purse, no increment for top 30% employees'. https://www.ndtvprofit.com/business/flipkart-tightens-purse-no-increment-for-top-30-employees.

News18 (2022): 'Flipkart to shut down its payment gateway PayZippy'. https://www.news18.com/news/india/flipkart-to-shut-down-its-payment-gateway-payzippy-710776.html. Accessed on 24 February 2022.

Nguyen, L. (2009): 'Research Methodology', in L. Nguyen (ed.), *Guerilla Capitalism: The State in the Market in Vietnam*, Chandos Publishing, 29–39. ISBN 978-1-84334-550-3.

Nightingale, A.J. (2020): 'Triangulation', in A. Kobayashi (ed.), *International Encyclopedia of Human Geography*, Second Edition, 477–480. ISBN 9780081022962.

Nilekani, N. (2016): 'Flipkart took off because it brought in cash on delivery', *The Economic Times*, August 16. https://economictimes.indiatimes.com/small-biz/start-ups/flipkart-took-off-because-it-brought-in-cash-on-delivery-nandan-nilekani/articleshow/53533483.cms.

Ninjacart Media: https://www.ninjacart.com/media/.

Onmanorama (2024): 'Flipkart may reduce workforce by up to 7%, affecting 1,500 employees'. https://www.onmanorama.com/news/business/2024/01/08/1500-employees-may-lose-lose-jobs-as-flipkart-plans-to-cut-workforce.html.

Palinkas, L., S.M. Horwitz, C.A. Green, J.P. Wisdom, N. Duan, and K. Hoagwood (2015): 'Purposeful Sampling for Qualitative Data Collection and Analysis in Mixed Method Implementation Research', *Adm Policy Mental Health*, 42 (5), 533–544. Doi:10.1007/s10488-013-0528-y.

Parker, S.K., and C.G. Collins (2010): 'Taking Stock: Integrating and Differentiating Multiple Proactive Behaviors', *Journal of Management*, 36, 633–662.

Parker, S.K., H.M. Williams, and N. Turner (2006): 'Modeling the Antecedents of Proactive Behavior at Work', *Journal of Applied Psychology*, 91 (3), 636–652.

Paunovic, S., and I.C. Dima (2014): 'Organizational Culture and Corporate Entrepreneurship', *Annals of the University of Petrosani, Economics*, 14 (1), 269–276.

Peer, N (2015): 'Flipkart acquires mobile ad network AdIQuity', *VCCircle*, March 7. https://www.vccircle.com/flipkart-acquires-mobile-ad-network-adiquity. Accessed on 12 March 2022.

Pitchiah, V. (2017): 'Flipkart launches "buy now, pay later" feature', *VCCircle*, June 19. https://www.vccircle.com/flipkart-launches-buy-now-pay-later-feature. Accessed on 28 March 2022.

PrivateCircle.com (2022): *Database*, 2022.

Rajan, T (2020): 'The Flipkart Story in India: From the Start to Walmart', *Asian Journal of Management Cases*, April 29. https://doi.org/10.1177%2F0972820120914526.

Rath (2022): 'List of All the Start-ups Acquired by Flipkart'. https://start-uptalky.com/flipkart-subsidiaries/.

Rauch, A., J. Wiklund, G.T. Lumpkin, and E. Frese (2009): 'Entrepreneurial Orientation and Business Performance: An Assessment of Past Research and Suggestions for the Future', *Entrepreneurship Theory & Practice*, May, 761–787.

Russell, J. (2017): 'Flipkart backs parenting network Tinystep with $2 million investment', Tech Crunch, January 18. https://techcrunch.com/2017/01/17/flipkart-baby-steps-tinystep-2-million/. Accessed on 26 March 2022.

Russell, R., and C. Russell (1992): 'An Examination of the Effects of Organizational Norms, Organizational Structure and Environmental Uncertainty on Entrepreneurial Strategy', *Journal of Management*, 18 (4), 639–656.

Saikind, N.J. (2010): 'Triangulation', in N.J. Saikind (ed.): *Encyclopedia of Research Design*, Sage Publications, New Delhi. DOI: https://dx.doi.org/10.4135/9781412961288.n469.

Sakhdari, K. (2016): 'Corporate Entrepreneurship: A Review and Future Research Agenda', *Technology Innovation Management Review*, 6 (8), 5–13.

Salkind, N.A. (2010): 'Triangulation', in *Encyclopedia of Research Design*, Sage Publications. DOI: https://dx.doi.org/10.4135/9781412961288.n469. Accessed on 22 June 2022.

Sareen, P (2017): 'How the Flipkart mafia flipped the fate of the Indian startup ecosystem', *Inc47*, May 17. https://inc42.com/features/flipkart-mafia/. Accessed on 4 April 2022.

Sareen, P (2014): 'Flipkart invests in ngpay, will shut down PayZippy', *Inc42*, September 1. https://inc42.com/buzz/flipkart-invests-ngpay-will-shutdown-payzippy/. Accessed on 24 February 2022.

Sarkar, J. (2021): 'Flipkart raises $3.6 billion fresh funds at $37.6 billion valuation', *The Times of India*, July 13. https://timesofindia.indiatimes.com/business/india-business/flipkart-raises-3-6-billion-fresh-funds-at-37-6-billion-valuation/articleshow/84364834.cms. Accessed on 14 April 2022.

Schaeffer, V. (2015): 'Corporate Entrepreneurship and Creativity in Large Firms: The Practice of Start-up Contests', *Journal of Innovation Economics & Management*, 3, 25–50.

Shepherd, D.A., H. Patzelt, and J.M. Haynie (2010):'Entrepreneurial Spirals: Deviation – Amplifying Lops of an Entrepreneurial

Mindset and Organizational Culture', *Entrepreneurship Theory and Practice*, 34 (1), 59–82.

Sharma, S. (2012): 'Flipkart buys electronics retailer Letsbuy for $25m'. https://timesofindia.indiatimes.com/business/india-business/Flipkart-buys-electronics-retailer-Letsbuy-for-25m/articleshow/11831516.cms.

Shrivastava, A. (2020): 'Flipkart Wholesale launches service in three cities', *The Economic Times*, September 2. https://economictimes.indiatimes.com/corporate/flipkart-wholesale-launches-service-in-3-cities/articleshow/77888801.cms?from=mdr. Accessed on 10 April 2022.

Shrivastava, A. (2019): 'Flipkart partners with Authentic Brands to license and distribute Nautca in India', *The Economic Times*, August 29. https://economictimes.indiatimes.com/small-biz/start-ups/newsbuzz/flipkart-partners-with-authentic-brands-to-license-and-distribute-nautica-in-india/articleshow/70885668.cms?from=mdr. Accessed on 6 April 2022.

Shirvastava, A., and M. Chanchani (2015): 'Flipkart, Tiger Global team up to invest Rs. 76 crore in online home rental start-up Nestaway', *The Economic Times*, July 22. https://economictimes.indiatimes.com/small-biz/start-ups/flipkart-tiger-global-team-up-to-invest-rs-76-crore-in-online-home-rental-start-up-nestaway/articleshow/48166593.cms. Accessed on 3 March 2022.

Singh, D. (2021): 'Flipkart enters crowded healthtech sector with SastaSundar acquisition', *The Economic Times*, November 21. https://economictimes.indiatimes.com/tech/start-ups/flipkart-enters-crowded-healthtech-sector-with-sastasundar-acquisition/articleshow/87797270.cms. Accessed on 16 April 2022.

Singh, M. (2019): 'Flipkart leads $60M investment in logistics start-up Shadowfax'. https://techcrunch.com/2019/12/05/shadowfax-flipkart/.

Singh, V. (2015): 'Flipkart & Accel Partners Backs Transportation Booking Marketplace Zinka Logistics With $6 Mn Funding'. https://inc42.com/flash-feed/zinka-logistics-raises-6-mn/.

Soni, A. (2015): 'Flipkart acquires Appiterate, to further strengthen its mobile offerings', *Your Story*, April 29. https://yourstory.com/2015/04/flipkart-acquires-appiterate/amp. Accessed on 10 March 2022.

Sreekumar, V. (2019): 'How Jeeves and F1 deliver on Flipkart's "Customer First" promise', *Flipkart Stories*, February 06. https://stories.flipkart.com/jeeves-f1-customer-first/. Accessed on 30 March 2022.

Start-up Genome (2022): *Start-up Ecosystem Report 2021*, USA.

Startupindia (2022a): https://www.start-upindia.gov.in/content/sih/en/start-upgov/start-up-recognition-page.html. Government of India, New Delhi. Accessed on 27 June 2022.

Startupindia (2022b): 'Start-up Ecosystem in India: Quick Facts'. https://www.start-upindia.gov.in/content/sih/en/international/go-to-market-guide/indian-start-up-ecosystem.html. Government of India, New Delhi. Accessed on 17 June 2022.

Start-up Talky (2022): 'List of 111 Unicorn Start-ups in India: 2022 Updated'. https://start-uptalky.com/top-unicorn-start-ups-india/#:~:text=Flipkart%20was%20among%20the%20first,was%20the%20first%20Indian%20unicorn. Accessed on 15 July 2022.

Talgeri, K. (2022): How Flipkart and Ninjacart discovered a win-win partnership over 18 months. https://yourstory.com/2022/01/flipkart-ninjacart-discovered-win-win-partnership#:~:text=In%20December%202021%2C%20 Walmart%20and,the%20ecommerce%20giant%20drives%20 demand.

Team Flipkart Stories (2021): 'Flipkart Ventures is the crystallization of our corporate development journey'. https://stories.flipkart.com/flipkart-ventures-corporate-development-ravi-iyer/.

Teng, B.S. (2007): 'Corporate Entrepreneurship Activities through Strategic Alliances: A Resource-Based Approach toward Competitive Advantage', *Journal of Management Studies*, 44 (1), 121–140.

The Economic Times (2022): 'Flipkart forays into healthcare sector; launches Flipkart Health Plus app', April 6. https://economictimes.indiatimes.com/industry/healthcare/biotech/healthcare/flipkart-forays-into-healthcare-sector-launches-flipkart-health-plus-app/articleshow/90691700.cms. Accessed on 20 April 2022.

The Next Web (2018): 'Dubbed the "iTunes of India", Flipkart's new music store takes Flyte'. https://thenextweb.com/news/dubbed-the-itunes-of-india-flipkarts-new-music-store-takes-flyte.

Thomson, N., and P. McNamara (2001): 'Achieving Post-Acquisition Success: The Role of Corporate Entrepreneurship', *Long Range Planning*, 34, 669–697.

Thornberry, N. (2001): 'Corporate Entrepreneurship: Antidote or Oxymoron?', *European Management Journal*, 5, 526–533.

Times of India (2014a): 'Flipkart, Myntra merge in Rs 2,000 crore deal'. https://timesofindia.indiatimes.com/tech-news/flipkart-myntra-merge-in-rs-2000-crore-deal/articleshow/35493912.cms?from=mdr.

Times of India-PTI (2019): 'Flipkart invests in EasyRewardz'. https://timesofindia.indiatimes.com/business/india-business/flipkart-invests-in-easyrewardz/articleshow/72125708.cms.

Tribbitt, M. (2017): 'Developing Entrepreneurial Behavior in Established Firms', *Graziadio Business Review*, 20 (2), 1–11.

Tseng, C., and C.C. Tseng (2019): 'Corporate Entrepreneurship as a Strategic Approach for Internal Innovation Performance', *Asia Pacific Journal of Innovation and Entrepreneurship*, 13 (1), 108–120.

Turner, T., and P. Pennington III, (2014): 'Organizational Networks and the Process of Corporate Entrepreneurship: How the Motivation, Opportunity, and Ability to Act Affect Firm Knowledge, Learning, and Innovation', *Small Business Economics*, 45: 447–463.

Turro, A., D. Urbano, and M. Peris-Ortiz (2014): 'Culture and Innovation: The Moderating Effect of Cultural Values on Corporate Entrepreneurship', *Technological Forecasting & Social Change*, 88, 360–369.

UNDP (United Nations Development Programme) (2001): *Human Development Report 2001*, Oxford University Press, New York.

Unger, J.M., A. Rauch, M. Frese, and N. Rosenbusch (2011): 'Human Capital and Entrepreneurial Success: A Meta-Analytical Review', *Journal of Business Venturing*, 26 (3), 341–358.

Varun (2020a): 'Story of Flipkart: How Sachin Bansal and Binny Bansal built India's leading ecommerce start-up', *The Indian Wire*, May 15. https://www.theindianwire.com/start-ups/flipkart-sachin-bansal-binny-bansal-268867/. Accessed on 12 February 2022.

Varun (2020b): 'Books to billions: How Sachin and Binny

Bansal built Flipkart to 100+ million customers'. https://medium.com/@varun.guru007/books-to-billions-how-sachin-and-binny-bansal-built-flipkart-to-100-million-customers-1447a68c338.

Reuters (2011): 'Flipkart acquires content from Bollywood news site Chakpak.com', Reuters, November 24. https://www.reuters.com/article/trivone-digital-services-acquires-wheels-idINDEE84H0CJ20120518/. Accessed on 12 February 2022.

VC Circle (2011): 'Flipkart raises $20m from Tiger Global in Series C Funding'. https://www.vccircle.com/flipkart-raises-20m-tiger-global-series-c-funding.

VC Circle (2014): 'Flipkart says it has hit annual revenue run rate of $1b in GMV'. https://www.vccircle.com/flipkart-says-it-has-hit-annual-revenue-run-rate-1b-gmv.

Venture Intelligence (2021): 'Indian unicorns: Highlights on India's $1-bn+ valued start-ups', Venture Intelligence (TSJ Media Pvt. Ltd), Chennai.

Venugopal, B (2017): 'How Happy and Flipkart birthed the Flipkart Kids', *Flipkart Stories*, August 31. https://stories.flipkart.com/happy-flipkart-kids/. Accessed on 16 February 2022.

Verma, S. (2016): 'Flipkart's Myntra acquires Jabong in $70 million "discount" deal', *Mint*, July 26. https://www.livemint.com/Companies/iicvIYFijqp9VRAx0ON46I/Flipkarts-Myntra-acquires-Jabong.html. Accessed on 14 March 2022.

Vikas, S.N. (2011): 'Watch out Amazon, Flipkart enters digital distribution space with Mime360 acquisition', *Techin Asia*, October 12. https://www.techinasia.com/flipkart-mime360-acquisition Accessed on 20th February 2022.

Walmart Press Release (2018): 'Walmart to invest in Flipkart Group, India's innovative ecommerce company'. https://

corporate.walmart.com/news/2018/05/09/walmart-to-invest-in-flipkart-group-indias-innovative-ecommerce-company.

Walmart Press Release (2021): 'Flipkart raises US$3.6 billion in funding'. :https://corporate.walmart.com/news/2021/07/12/flipkart-raises-us-3-6-billion-in-funding-to-accelerate-the-growth-of-the-consumer-internet-ecosystem-in-india.

Wei, L., and Y. Ling (2014): 'CEO Characteristics and Corporate Entrepreneurship in Transition Economies: Evidence from China', *Journal of Business Research*, 68: 1157–1165.

Whittingham, M.J., P.A. Stephens, R.B. Bradbury, and R.P. Freckleton (2006): 'Why Do We Still Use Stepwise Modelling in Ecology and Behavior?', *Journal of Animal Ecology*, Volume 75, 1182–1189.

WION web (2018): 'Flipkart's first employee was hired at Rs.8,000 a month. Today he is a multi-millionaire', May 9. https://www.wionews.com/india-news/flipkarts-1st-employee-was-hired-at-rs-8000-a-month-today-hes-a-multi-millionaire-135789. Accessed on 24 April 2022.

Yang, Z., R. Li-Hua, X. Zhang, and Y. Wang (2007): 'Corporate Entrepreneurship and Market Performance: An Empirical Study in China', *Journal of Technology Management in China*, 2 (2), 154–162.

Your Story (2015): 'Top E-Commerce Acquisitions in India in 2015', June 26. https://yourstory.com/2015/06/ecommerce-acquisition-india-2015/amp. Accessed on 12 February 2022.

YourStory: Binny Bansal: https://yourstory.com/people/binny-bansal.

Zahra, S.A., and J.G. Covin (1995): 'Contextual Influences on the Corporate Entrepreneurship-Performance Relationship: A Longitudinal Analysis', *Journal of Business Venturing*, 10, 43–58.

Zeegers, M., and D. Barron (2015): *Milestone Moments in Getting your Ph.D. in Qualitative Research*, Chandos Publishing, ISBN 978-0-08-100231-5.

Zimmerman, J. (2010): 'Corporate Entrepreneurship at GE and Intel', *Journal of Business Case Studies*, 6 (5), 77–82.

Ziyae, B., and H. Sadeghi (2021): 'Exploring Relationship between Corporate Entrepreneurship and Firm Performance: The Mediating Effect of Strategic Entrepreneurship', *Baltic Journal of Management*, 16 (1), 113–133.